CW01102978

Entrepreneurial Crisis Management

Sukanlaya Sawang

Entrepreneurial Crisis Management

How Small and Micro-Firms Prepare for and Respond to Crises

palgrave
macmillan

Sukanlaya Sawang
Coventry University
Coventry, UK

QUT Business School
Queensland University of Technology
Brisbane, Australia

ISBN 978-3-031-25187-0   ISBN 978-3-031-25188-7   (eBook)
https://doi.org/10.1007/978-3-031-25188-7

© The Author(s), under exclusive licence to Springer Nature Switzerland AG 2023

This work is subject to copyright. All rights are solely and exclusively licensed by the Publisher, whether the whole or part of the material is concerned, specifically the rights of translation, reprinting, reuse of illustrations, recitation, broadcasting, reproduction on microfilms or in any other physical way, and transmission or information storage and retrieval, electronic adaptation, computer software, or by similar or dissimilar methodology now known or hereafter developed.

The use of general descriptive names, registered names, trademarks, service marks, etc. in this publication does not imply, even in the absence of a specific statement, that such names are exempt from the relevant protective laws and regulations and therefore free for general use.

The publisher, the authors, and the editors are safe to assume that the advice and information in this book are believed to be true and accurate at the date of publication. Neither the publisher nor the authors or the editors give a warranty, expressed or implied, with respect to the material contained herein or for any errors or omissions that may have been made. The publisher remains neutral with regard to jurisdictional claims in published maps and institutional affiliations.

This Palgrave Macmillan imprint is published by the registered company Springer Nature Switzerland AG.
The registered company address is: Gewerbestrasse 11, 6330 Cham, Switzerland

Preface

The word "crisis" has been used to describe many different situations in life, from personal relationship and health problems all the way up to global events such as natural disasters or a pandemic. Equally, crisis has become a common word in business and management, with crisis management having become a standard phrase that most, if not all, larger organizations have incorporated. Crisis management in small and micro firms however has been a largely overlooked topic that requires more exploration to fully understand. On the one hand, for small businesses, the decision to respond to a crisis event can be more agile and can be done swiftly, without the process being bogged down by layers of bureaucracy, compared to larger organizations. However, decisions made by a single person (small business owner-manager) can be biased, unfounded, or hasty, and may not always be in the best interests of the company. Small business owners may make decisions to respond to a crisis based on emotion, rather than logic. This can be a recipe for disaster, as emotions can change quickly and unexpectedly. This book offers some guidance for scholars and practitioners, including small business owners to understand better the concept, limitations, and considerations of crisis management, specifically in the small business context. In this book, it will be demonstrated that there is no single solution for a small business to cope with a crisis. Nonetheless, there are some common methods and frameworks that have emerged from past experiences.

This book consists of four chapters. Chapter 1 aims to provide a background to and framework for crisis management. The first chapter is fundamental knowledge for readers (especially for those who are new to the crisis management) to gain a basic understanding of the concept of crisis management. Chapter 2 shifts the focus of this book to crisis management in the small business context. This chapter draws from two key theoretical frameworks (Social Capital and Business Continuity) to discuss the crisis management principals within a small business context. Chapter 3 centers on a major crisis event which had a worldwide impact: the COVID-19 pandemic. This chapter both discusses how the event has impacted on small businesses, as well as how small businesses have coped through crisis management with the event. The chapter highlights core facilitating factors that aided small businesses' resilience, and how they managed to revitalize their businesses. It will also shed light on small business owners' wellbeing after the crisis. Chapter 4 discusses ways forward for crisis management in small businesses.

In today's business world, it is more important than ever to be prepared for a crisis event. Whether it is a natural disaster, a terrorist attack, or simply an interruption in the supply chain, even small businesses must be ready to respond. While this book cannot offer the perfect solution to every problem, it provides a framework and examples to help better understand the context, and to offer pathways to develop an effective crisis plan for small businesses. By understanding how to manage a crisis, small businesses can reduce the impact of potentially devastating events.

Coventry, UK   Sukanlaya Sawang

Contents

1 Understanding Crisis Management in Modern Societies   1

2 Crisis Management and Small Businesses   17

3 COVID-19 and Small Businesses Responses   41

4 Forward Looking   59

Index   73

1
Understanding Crisis Management in Modern Societies

Abstract A crisis is a challenging and pivotal moment with the potential to cause disruption and destruction. Crisis management is essential in minimizing potential damage and assisting with quicker recovery. Understanding the definition and history of crisis and crisis management is essential for dealing with crises in an effective way. In this chapter 'crisis' is defined, and the stages of crises are discussed beyond the traditional stages of pre-crisis, crisis, and post-crisis. In the second half of the chapter the individual versus organizational perspectives of crisis are discussed, followed with the crisis level of impact on organizational context.

Keywords Crisis management • Crisis stages • Individual crisis • Organizational crisis

1 Defining Crisis

A crisis is typically defined as a turning point or situation of great importance that requires an immediate response. Crises can be personal, such as a health-related condition or a loss of a job, or they can be global, such as a natural disaster or an act of terrorism. In either case, a crisis can have far-reaching consequences and can often lead to feelings of anxiety and insecurity with individuals.

Crisis theory has its roots in the economic work of German sociologist Karl Marx. Loosely paraphrased, he argued that history would be a series of class struggles between those in power and those without it, the working class, or "proletariat" (Marx & Engels, 1848). His belief lead him eventually to come up with an idea for how these conflicts could lead themselves into revolutions where workers overthrow their capitalists' masters after they have finished fighting one another over who has less privilege within society at large. While Marx's work was primarily concerned with economic crises, his ideas about class conflict and revolution have been applied to other types of crises as well, including political and social crises. Crisis theory from an economic perspective, concerning the causes and consequences of the tendency for the rate of profit to fall in a capitalist system, is associated with the Marxian critique of political economy, and was further popularized through Marxist economics.

Following the extensive setbacks to independent working-class politics, the widespread destruction both of people, property and capital value, the 1930s and 1940s saw attempts to reformulate Marx's work with less revolutionary consequences, for example in Joseph Schumpeter's concept of creative destruction and his presentation of Marx's crisis theory as a prefiguration of aspects of what Schumpeter, and others, championed as merely a theory of business cycles. Keynesians argue that a "crisis" may refer to an especially sharp bust cycle of the regular boom and bust pattern of "chaotic" capitalist development, which, if no countervailing action is taken, could continue to develop into a recession or depression.

Moving away from purely economic crises, Caplan (1964) simply defines a crisis as "a situation in which the expected value of all future outcomes is negative". In other words, a crisis is a period of time during which the future looks bleak. This could be due to an economic recession, but also due to natural disasters, or any number of other factors and events. Crises are often caused by irrational behavior or external circumstances, which can make them difficult to predict or prevent. Nonetheless, it is possible to minimize the damage caused by crises through careful planning, preparation, and execution. Caplan's crisis theory posits that crises are caused by a combination of *preconditions, triggers,* and *dynamic processes.* Preconditions are those conditions which increase the likelihood of a crisis occurring, while triggers are those events which precipitate a crisis. Dynamic processes refer to the ways in which a crisis unfolds and intensifies. Caplan argues that crises are best understood as the product of all three of these factors. Caplan's theory has been widely influential and it has been used to explain a wide variety of historical crises, from the French Revolution to the collapse of the Soviet Union. However, it has also been criticized on several grounds. Some have argued that it overemphasizes the role of external factors in causing crises, while others have contended that it does not adequately account for the role of human agency. Nevertheless, Caplan's crisis theory remains an important contribution to our understanding of how and why crises occur.

In the field of organizational psychology, crisis refers to a specific type of event that can have a profound and lasting impact on an organization. According to Milburn et al. (1983), a crisis is "an abnormal and unpredictable event or set of events that threatens the continued existence or performance of an organization" (p. 1141). Crises can have a number of different impacts on organizations. In some cases, they can lead to drastic changes in strategy or operations. In other cases, they can cause short-term disruptions that eventually stabilize. And in some cases, crises can be so damaging that they lead to the death of an organization. The impact of a crisis will depend on a number of factors, including the severity of the event, the preparedness of the organization, and the reaction of key stakeholders.

The ability to effectively manage crises is becoming increasingly important in today's business world. Organizations need to understand what a crisis is, how it can affect their businesses and business owners, and the best strategies for responding. With this understanding, companies can be better prepared when a crisis arises, enabling them to quickly respond in an effective way. By having a clear understanding of what constitutes a crisis, businesses can be better prepared to deal with them when they occur.

2 Crisis Stages: Individual Perspective

When an organization or individual faces a crisis, it is important to understand the different stages that may be experienced. From the individual perspective, people in a crisis may feel confused, disoriented, and are unable to think clearly. They may also feel like they are in danger or under threat. Halpern (1973) explains that there are three stages of a crisis: pre-crisis, crisis, and post-crisis. During the pre-crisis stage, an individual may be under stress, but is still functioning relatively well. However, at some point, the stress becomes too much and the individual moves into the crisis stage. This is when they start to experience some of the symptoms mentioned above. Finally, in the post-crisis stage, the individual starts to recover and returns to their normal mode of functioning.

Caplan (1964) proposed that there are four main stages in a crisis reaction: impact, denial, mobilization, and resolution. The first stage, impact, is when an individual is confronted with a traumatic event. This can be a physical or psychological shock, and it can often lead to a state of disbelief. In the second stage, denial, individuals may try to minimize the severity of the event or convince themselves that it did not happen, or at least did not have a major impact. This can be a defense mechanism that helps people to cope with the stress of the situation. The third stage, mobilization, is when individuals begin to act in order to cope with the crisis. This may involve seeking help from others, or making plans to protect oneself. Finally, the fourth stage, resolution, is when individuals have accepted the event and are beginning to move past and on with their lives. This process can often be difficult and may take months or even years to complete. However, it is important to remember that each individual reacts differently to crisis situations and there is no one correct way to deal with them.

3 Crisis Stages: Organizational Perspective

An organizational crises can be seen as a 'low probability-high impact' events that threatens the viability of an organization, or part of an organization. They are characterized by ambiguity in cause and effect along with a belief that decisions need to be made swiftly because time is scarce for those involved (Pearson & Clair, 1998). In organizational context, there are generally four stages to organizational crisis response (Appelbaum et al., 2012). These stages are pre-crisis, crisis, post-crisis, and normalization. Each stage has its own unique characteristics and challenges, and requires a different response from the organization. The pre-crisis stage is characterized by a period of relative calm. During this time, it is important for organizations to take steps to prepare for possible crises, such as conducting risk assessments and developing contingency plans. The crisis stage is when the actual crisis occurs. This is when organizations must spring into action and implement their contingency plans, or quickly develop these. The post-crisis stage is characterized by a period of recovery and reflection. During this time, organizations should reflect to understand what went well and what could be improved for future crises. Finally, the normalization stage is when things return to business as usual. However, it is important to remain vigilant during this time, as another crisis could occur at any moment.

Any organization or individual can face a crisis at any time. It is important to understand the different stages that may be experienced during a crisis. Although there are some similarities between the two perspectives, it is important to understand the distinct stages that may be experienced from both an organizational and an individual perspective.

4 Crisis Level and Organizational Impacts

Scholars have long recognized that crises come in different shapes and sizes, with varying levels of severity and impact. Rapoport and Anatol (1960) proposed a classification system for crises based on three key factors: type of event, number of casualties, and duration. This typology is useful for understanding the range of potential outcomes that can result from a crisis. Their framework demonstrates that some events (e.g., natural disasters) are more likely to cause fatalities than others are (e.g., labor disputes). However, this view is less helpful for understanding how different types of crises evolve over time. For instance, the framework does not account for the fact that some crises (e.g., terrorist attacks, earthquakes, flash-flooding) tend to occur instantly, while others (e.g., financial meltdowns, climate change) can unfold more slowly. Then, Baldwin (1978) took a slightly different approach, arguing that crises can be distinguished based on action, relation, and event. According to this framework, organizations perceive crises as arising from either an increase in the number or the magnitude of relevant actions; a change in the relations between organization and environment, including stakeholders; or deterioration of some environmental event.

Another framework is proposed by Shrivastava (1993), identifying four key elements. Shrivastava names these four elements as causes, consequences, caution, and coping. The causes element encompasses all factors that lead to the crisis event. The consequences element refers to the (negative) outcomes that results from the crisis. The caution component highlights the need for organizations to be prepared for future crises. The coping element emphasizes the importance of effective coping mechanisms in times of crisis. This framework provides a systematic way of thinking about, and responding to crises, but just as the first framework, it does not discuss the magnitude or severity of a crisis.

In the organizational context, it is vital to have a system in place for how an organization handles situation that require rapid response and careful judgement. The severity of the crisis is an important factor that dictates the steps companies need to take in order to mitigate the damages. Therefore, it is essential to have a good understanding of how to measure the severity of a crisis. Zhou et al. (2019) provide a detailed framework for evaluating the severity of a crisis. Their work discusses three dimensions of severity: impact, likelihood, and credibility. Impact refers to how serious the consequences of the crisis would be. For example, if a company were to experience a data breach, the impact could range from customers being inconvenienced to them suffering significant financial losses. Likelihood refers to the probability that the crisis will occur. For example, if a company has experienced several data breaches in the past, it is more likely to experience another one in the future, unless action is taken. Credibility refers to how believable the company's response to the crisis would be. For example, if a company's response is viewed as being inadequate or dishonest, it could damage the company's credibility. These three dimensions are important considerations when assessing the severity of an organizational crisis. In conclusion, crisis classification frameworks have evolved over time, offering varying levels of insight into different kinds of crises. However, it is essential to have a good understanding of how to measure the severity of a crisis in order to effectively respond. By taking into account these mentioned factors at the outset, organizations can be better prepared to cope with any potential crisis that may arise.

5 Multidisciplinary View on Crisis

Crisis management can no longer be viewed through a linear lens. Instead, it must become a more holistic approach that looks to understand the driving forces behind crises and how they can best be managed. This means looking at the psychological, sociological-policy, and technological structures involved to help shape the most effective crisis plan (Pearson & Clair, 1998). It also means understanding how these various elements interact and inform one another to better prepare for, assess, prevent and manage crises. Only when we look beyond the traditional narrative of crisis management can we begin to truly understand how to effectively tackle them in the future.

5.1 Crisis from a Psychological Perspective

Within the psychology dimension, a crisis can be defined as a situation where there is a designated threat to an individual or group, and a response is required to neutralize that threat. Drawing from Lazarus (1987) work of the Transactional theory suggests that individuals tend to appraise their situation using three main criteria: novelty, threat, and coping potential. Novelty refers to how new or unexpected the situation is, threat pertains to any potential harm posed by the crisis, and coping potential revolves around an individual's capacity for resilience in reacting to and managing the situation. Consequently, an effective response requires a thorough understanding of these criteria in order to neutralize the threat. Applying these insights to a business context, if business owners perceive their situation as being new and threatening, but also believes that they have the ability to cope with it, they are less likely to experience a crisis. On the other hand, if they perceive their situation as being familiar and non-threatening, or believe that they do not have the ability to cope with it, they are more likely to experience a crisis. While cognitive theories provide valuable insights into how individuals react to crisis situations, they are not always able to explain or predict all of the individual forces involved. However, by taking into account both cognitive and psychoanalytic perspectives (Freud, 2014), researchers can gain a more complete understanding of how and why individuals experience, and respond to a crisis.

5.2 Crisis from a Social-Political Perspective

In a social-political context, crises typically arise when there is disagreement or discord between different factions within a society (Boin & Renaud, 2013). This can lead to unstable conditions that can erupt into violence or other forms of civil unrest. Political crises often involve corruption, power struggles, or the misuse of authority, which can cause further divisions among people and create an environment of fear and mistrust. In times of crisis, it is essential for different social and political groups to work together to find a resolution. Otherwise, the situation can rapidly deteriorate, leading to disastrous consequences. In recent years, there has been an increased interest in the social and political aspects of crisis management. In particular, scholars have debated the role of the state in responding to crises and the impact of crisis on social and political institutions. Habermas (1975) argues that the state has a responsibility to protect citizens from harm, while O'Connor (1987) suggests that the state is responsible for ensuring accessibility to critical resources.

Hurst (1995) goes even further, arguing that crises can have a profound impact on social and political institutions, often leading to their collapse. While each of these theorists offers a different perspective on the role of the state in crisis management, they all suggest that the state plays an important role in protecting citizens during times of crisis.

5.3 Crisis from a Technological-Structural Perspective

Technology has become an integral part of our lives, and yet it can be seen as a crisis on itself. In a world where technology is advancing at an ever-increasing rate, the potential risks of technological advancement are becoming increasingly visible. From cyber-security breaches, to data manipulations and Artificial Intelligence (AI) driven automation, technology presents both opportunities and dangers. Furthermore, the way in which technology interacts with social structures in creating inequalities can also be seen as a crisis. These structurally embedded issues become more severe with increased use of new technologies such as artificial intelligence and machine learning algorithms, with their lack of transparency potentially resulting in further marginalization of certain groups. Technological-structural perspective views modern technology is so complex and tightly coupled that even small problems can lead to cascading failures. This view has been supported by subsequent research on a variety of crises, including the 1980s nuclear meltdown at Chernobyl, the failure of the Space Shuttle Challenger, and the 9/11 terrorist attacks (Pauchant & Douville, 1993). The recent increase in usage of AI and machine learning algorithms has further exposed us to such risks, as data manipulation, lack of transparency and inequality embedded within these technologies are becoming more visible. While technological-structural views on crisis are helpful in understanding how and why crises occur, they also have limitations. For one, this perspective does not account for human factors, such as errors, that can contribute to technological failures. Additionally, this view does not always explain why some crises are more severe than others. Despite these limitations, the technological-structural perspective remains a valuable tool for understanding how and why crises occur.

6 Organizational Sensemaking of Crisis

The sensemaking theory (Weick, 1993) has been widely used to understand how organizations make sense of crises. Weick argued that sensemaking is the continual process of orienting oneself in one's surroundings and making sense of one's experiences. In crisis situations, this process is often enacted unconsciously and rapidly, as organizations attempt to make sense of their rapidly changing environment and adapt their behavior accordingly. Weick proposed that there are four key elements of sensemaking in crisis situations: identity, meaning, continuity, and saliency. Identity refers to the need to establish who is involved in the situation and what role they play. Meaning refers to the need to understand the significance of the event and how it fits into the wider context. Continuity refers to the need to maintain a sense of order and coherence in a chaotic situation. Saliency refers to the need to identify which aspects of the situation are most salient and warrant attention first. Weick argued that these four elements are interdependent, and that successful sensemaking in a crisis requires all four to be considered simultaneously. The challenge for organizations is to create systems and structures that supporting rapid and effective sensemaking in crisis situations.

Organizations are constantly subjected to tremendous amounts of pressure and stress, which can eventually lead to crisis. To effectively deal with crisis, it is important for organizations to have a clear understanding of sensemaking. Maitlis and Sonenshein (2010) suggest that sensemaking involves three main aspects: (1) attending to the situation, (2) making sense of the situation, and (3) taking action. These steps are not always sequential, but rather they represent an ongoing loop as individuals continually refine their understanding of the situation and take action accordingly. This process is often recursive, with individuals cycling through the steps multiple times, as they try to make sense of a complex and ever-changing world. By understanding the sensemaking process, individuals can more effectively navigate times of crisis or change.

Combe and Carrington's (2015) work on sensemaking under crisis supplements broader frameworks on leader cognition during crisis (e.g. Weick, 1993). In their study of management teams during the 9/11 terrorist attacks, Combe and Carrington found that leaders engaged in three aspects: making sense of the situation, coordinating a response, and managing emotions. These activities were not isolated; rather, they were intertwined and constantly evolving as new information became available. Sensemaking was also shaped by the teams' prior experiences, which influenced how they interpreted and made sense of the situation. Ultimately, the work highlights the importance of leader cognition in crisis situations and how it can change over time as new information becomes available. This is valuable work that contributes to our understanding of how leaders make decisions during moments of crisis.

Drawing from the discussed work by Weick (1993), Maitlis and Sonenshein (2010), and Combe and Carrington (2015), organizational sensemaking can be viewed as a three-step process that helps individuals and groups make decisions in times of uncertainty. The first step is to identify the key issues and stakeholders involved. The second step is to make sense of the situation by gathering information and perspectives from different sources. The third step is to take action, which may involve coordinating a response or managing emotions. Common themes that emerge from this process include the need for timely and accurate information, the importance of stakeholder involvement, and the need for effective communication. By understanding these themes, organizations can more effectively navigate times of change and uncertainty.

In organizational context, the paradox of sensemaking refers to the conflicting goals of trying to make sense of an organization while also being part of that organization (Allard-Poesi, 2005). The problem is that, to understand an organization, one must distance oneself from it; but as soon as one tries to do so, one's status as a member of the organization affects one's ability to see it clearly. This creates a tension between different ways of looking at the organization—insider versus outsider, micro versus macro—that can be difficult to resolve. The paradox of sensemaking is further complicated by the fact that organizations are constantly changing, which makes it difficult to achieve a clear understanding of them. Nonetheless, it is important to try to make sense of organizations to improve their functioning.

Finally, the competing values framework is a model that categorizes organizations based on how they prioritize four main values: stability, flexibility, internal focus, and external focus (Cameron & Quinn, 1999). This framework can be used to better understand how organizations make sense of their surroundings and make decisions. For example, an organization that prioritizes stability and internal focus is likely to be more risk-averse and have a slower reaction time to changes in the environment. In contrast, an organization that prioritizes flexibility and external focus is likely to be more innovative and proactive. By understanding where an organization falls on the spectrum of these values, it is easier to predict how they will approach sensemaking. In conclusion, sensemaking is an important process that helps organizations and individuals respond to complex and rapidly changing environments. Understanding these processes can help organizations create structures that support effective decision-making during times of uncertainty.

7 The Role of Culture on Sensemaking of Crisis

Scholars have long debated the role of culture in crisis sensemaking. Some researchers maintain that cultural values play a significant role in shaping how individuals and groups react to crisis situations. Viewing culture through shared sensemaking suggests that within different cultures, those embedded within it seek out narratives to cope with a crisis in accordance with the values and beliefs already present within their culture (Sherman & Roberto, 2020). The narrative and culture are thus interwoven to create a seamless sensemaking message that supports the return of sensemaking. Accepting this role of culture within the context of crisis management, combined with the knowledge that each organization has its own culture, it makes sense to assume that organizations equally seek out narratives to cope with a crisis in accordance with the values and beliefs already present within their organizational culture.

In addition, culture also affects the way organizations communicate during a crisis (Fellows & Liu, 2016). For example, some organizational cultures may be more likely to use formal channels of communication, such as press releases, whereas others may rely more on informal channels, such as social media. This can impact the kind of information that is disseminated during a crisis, as well as how it is interpreted by those who receive it. Ultimately, culture plays a significant role in crisis sensemaking and this should be taken into account when responding to a crisis situation. The work of Russo et al. (2020) highlights the importance of semiotic cultural psychology theory in understanding the role of culture in crisis sensemaking. According to their work, culture manifests itself in three key ways: shared values and beliefs, common symbols and meanings, and shared patterns of behavior. These manifestations of culture influence how organizational members make sense of crises, and can lead to different responses to crisis situations. For example, shared values and beliefs may lead organizations to downplay the seriousness of a crisis, or symbolic meaning and sensemaking may be used to justify certain actions during a crisis. Therefore, understanding cultural norms is essential for effective sensemaking during times of crisis. A company's culture is likely to be shaped by its values, beliefs and practices which guide decision-making processes in uncertain circumstances. The role of culture in sensemaking is critical during times of crisis because it affects how individuals and organizations respond to uncertainty and make decisions about the future. Companies must be aware of cultural dynamics when making sense out of challenging circumstances in order to increase the chances of successful outcomes. By understanding the role of culture in crisis sensemaking, we can better understand how organizations interpret and respond to crises.

8 Conclusion

A crisis is a critical event that poses an immediate threat to an individual, group, or organization. Crisis management is the process of identifying, assessing, and responding to crises. Understanding the definition of crisis and the basic concepts of crisis management is important for individuals, groups, and organizations because it helps them to be better prepared to respond to crises effectively. In the wake of a crisis, it is essential to make sense of what has happened to develop an effective response. This process of understanding is known as organizational sensemaking. Organizational sensemaking is important because it helps leaders to identify the key issues that need to be addressed and to develop a plan of action. Additionally, organizational sensemaking helps organizations to learn from their experiences and prevent future crises. Without a clear understanding of what has happened, it is difficult to take steps to protect oneself or one's organization from future harm. Consequently, organizational sensemaking is a critical part of crisis management. The process of organizational sensemaking can be viewed as a cycle of four steps: gathering information, making sense of the information, taking action, and evaluating the results. This process is essential for organizations in today's rapidly changing environment. By constantly gathering information and making sense of it, organizations can adapt to new circumstances and make informed decisions about how to best achieve their goals. Taking action based on this analysis is crucial, but it is also important to evaluate the results of one's actions and learn from them. This cycle of sensemaking is an essential part of organizational success in a constantly changing world.

References

Allard-Poesi, F. (2005). The paradox of sensemaking in organizational analysis. *Organization, 12*(2), 169–196.

Appelbaum, S. H., Keller, S., Alvarez, H., & Bédard, C. (2012). Organizational crisis: Lessons from Lehman Brothers and Paulson & company. *International Journal of Commerce and Management, 22*(4), 286–305.

Baldwin, B. A. (1978). A paradigm for the classification of emotional crises: Implications for crisis intervention. *American Journal of Orthopsychiatry, 48*(3), 538–551.

Boin, A., & Renaud, C. (2013). Orchestrating joint sensemaking across government levels: Challenges and requirements for crisis leadership. *Journal of Leadership Studies, 7*(3), 41–46.

Cameron, K. S., & Quinn, R. E. (1999). *Diagnosing and changing organizational culture.* Addison Wesley.

Caplan, G. (1964). *Principles of preventive psychiatry*. Basic Books.
Combe, I. A., & Carrington, D. J. (2015). Leaders' sensemaking under crises: Emerging cognitive consensus over time within management teams. *The Leadership Quarterly, 26*(3), 307–322.
Fellows, R., & Liu, A. (2016). Sensemaking in the cross-cultural contexts of projects. *International Journal of Project Management, 34*(2), 246–257.
Freud, S. (2014). Psychoanalysis. In R. B. Ewen (Ed.), *An introduction to theories of personality* (pp. 11–51). Psychology Press.
Habermas, J. (1975). *Legitimation crisis*. Beacon Press.
Halpern, H. A. (1973). Crisis theory: A definitional study. *Community Mental Health Journal, 9*(4), 342–349.
Hurst, D. K. (1995). *Crisis & renewal*. Harvard Business School Press.
Lazarus, R. S. (1987). Stress and coping. In G. L. Maddox (Ed.), *The encyclopedia of aging* (pp. 647–649). Springer.
Maitlis, S., & Sonenshein, S. (2010). Sensemaking in crisis and change: Inspiration and insights from Weick (1988). *Journal of Management Studies, 47*(3), 551–580.
Marx, K., & Engels, F. (1848). *The communist manifesto* (D. McLellan, Ed.). Oxford University Press.
Milburn, T. W., Schuler, R. S., & Watman, K. H. (1983). Organizational crisis. Part I: Definition and conceptualization. *Human Relations, 36*(12), 1141–1160.
O'Connor, J. (1987). *The meaning of crisis: A theoretical introduction*. Basil Blackwell.
Pauchant, T. C., & Douville, R. (1993). Recent research in crisis management: A study of 24 authors' publications from 1986 to 1991. *Industrial & Environmental Crisis Quarterly, 7*(1), 43–66.
Pearson, C. M., & Clair, J. A. (1998). Reframing crisis management. *Academy of Management Review, 23*(1), 59–76.
Rapoport, A., & Anatol, R. (1960). *Fights, games, and debates*. University of Michigan Press.
Russo, F., Mannarini, T., & Salvatore, S. (2020). From the manifestations of culture to the underlying sensemaking process. The contribution of semiotic cultural psychology theory to the interpretation of socio-political scenario. *Journal for the Theory of Social Behaviour, 50*(3), 301–320.
Sherman, W. S., & Roberto, K. J. (2020). Are you talkin'to me?: The role of culture in crisis management sensemaking. *Management Decision, 58*(10), 2195–2211.

Shrivastava, P. (1993). Crisis theory/practice: Towards a sustainable future. *Industrial & Environmental Crisis Quarterly, 7*(1), 23–42.

Weick, K. E. (1993). The collapse of sensemaking in organizations: The Mann Gulch disaster. *Administrative Science Quarterly, 38*(4), 628–652.

Zhou, Z., Ki, E. J., & Brown, K. A. (2019). A measure of perceived severity in organizational crises: A multidimensional scale development and validation. *Journal of International Crisis and Risk Communication Research, 2*(1), 39–60.

2

Crisis Management and Small Businesses

Abstract This chapter unpacks the reasons why small businesses, as opposed to larger organizations, are more vulnerable to crises. It is also important to understanding how small businesses perceive, interpret, and respond to crises, through the sensemaking process. Sensemaking is the process of constructing meaning from available data and experiences. This involves understanding the risks associated with certain decisions, as well as being able to effectively utilize crisis management strategies after these risks have been identified. This chapter also introduces two key theories, 'social capital' and 'Business Continuity Management (BCM)' to better understand small businesses crisis management behaviors. Social capital refers to resources that are available through networks of relationships between people, such as mutual trust or shared values. BCM is a system of processes and controls designed to protect a company's critical business processes from disruption by accounting for potential problems stemming from natural disasters or other unexpected events. Utilizing the sensemaking process along with social capital and business continuity management can help reduce risk, aiding small businesses in overcoming any unforeseen challenges that may arise.

Keywords Sensemaking • Types of crises • Stakeholder management • Small business response

1 Small Businesses Are More Vulnerable to Crises

The small and medium enterprise (SME) sector has been an important part of economies worldwide. These companies are vital to both keeping the economy running, as well as leading innovation with their cutting-edge ideas that help shape new trends on a global scale. The prime economic generator that is SMEs is greatly vulnerable to a variety of risks including natural disasters, environmental disasters, and civic unrest. A crisis can often have both a negative and positive effects, in many different ways, upon the wider SME sector. Where some are struggling, others see opportunities. Opportunities may be unethical (price-gouging) as well as simply a result of circumstances (home-delivery businesses during the COVID-19 pandemic) and increased demand. The most common effects however lead to threats to the continued existence of a business (Doern et al., 2019). Others may require a business model update with new strategies for success (such as innovation or new market) (Breier et al., 2021), or present themselves through psychological impact among small business owners (Nguyen & Sawang, 2016; Sawang et al., 2020). SMEs are also more vulnerable to shocks and crises than larger businesses (Doern, 2016). This can be attributed to their size that makes them more susceptible to any unforeseen turn in the market or an emergency situation like natural disasters. Any major disruptions across different parts on society will as well affect SMEs negatively if not handled properly. Commonly, SMEs will have limited financial resources, as well as time constraints preventing thorough preparation beforehand. Although a study by Corey and Deitch (2011) found that, while business size does not seem to be related with organizational performance in crisis situations, larger businesses are more likely to have emergency response plans and are more likely to have taken pre-crises precautions. They also tend toward having better communication systems set up for when such events happen, which helps them reduce, for example, inventory loss during crisis times. While crisis management as an area has been well researched, crisis management within small businesses is an area that has yet been largely left unexplored. Large firms are well studied in their context, but how start-ups or small businesses manage a crisis remains unclear. The fragility of small business owners and their lack of resources is an often ignored reality in disaster response and recovery. Smaller companies are at risk for both natural disasters as well as man-made ones, which can easily lead them to close up shop when faced with insurmountable challenges like rising rent, insurance premiums, and recovery costs that regularly outweigh any benefits they might get from shutting down operations temporarily. This chapter thus aims to discuss the key theories that can mitigate the negative impact from crisis within the small business context.

2 Crisis Sensemaking Among Small Businesses

When discussing sensemaking and crisis, it is important to understand the difference between small and large businesses. Small businesses typically have limited resources and are less likely to have dedicated staff for crisis management. As often is the case in small businesses, one person will have multiple hats, and can be for example sales-manager, facilities-manager and crisis-manager all rolled into one, with the sales-manager being their primary role, and preparing for potential crises may not be high on their agenda. This can make it more difficult for small businesses to effectively manage a crisis. In contrast, well prepared large businesses typically have more resources dedicated, and are thus better equipped to handle a crisis. While both small and large businesses can benefit from using a sensemaking framework during a crisis, large businesses may be better able to effectively utilize this tool due to their greater resources. When applied to the realm of business, sensemaking is defined as "the process by which people give meaning to their experiences" (Weick, 1995, p. 22). This process is often driven by a need to make sense of ambiguous or chaotic situations.

1. Limited resources: One major challenge faced by small businesses during a crisis is limited resources. With fewer resources at their disposal, it can be difficult for small businesses to gather the information

and data needed to properly assess potential threats or respond appropriately. This can lead decision-makers to rely on personal experiences or gut instincts instead of hard data when determining how best to prepare or respond.
2. Lack of experience: Another obstacle is the lack of experience many small business owners have in dealing with crises. Entrepreneurs who run small businesses may not have had prior experience handling high-pressure situations, which can make it challenging for them to evaluate information accurately and make informed decisions that would minimize or mitigate the impact of a crisis.
3. Reliance on personal relationships: Small businesses also tend to rely heavily on personal relationships and networks. During a crisis, however, these relationships can be disrupted or strained, making communication and coordination difficult. This can hinder efforts to gather accurate information about what is happening and make effective decisions accordingly.
4. Limited knowledge availability: Due to their smaller size, many small businesses may have limited knowledge and expertise within their organization. This can result in decisions being made based on incomplete or inaccurate information, as there may not be enough people with relevant expertise available to provide guidance.

Despite these challenges, small businesses can still be successful in making sense of a crisis if they take the time to plan and prepare ahead of time. By identifying potential risks and developing contingency plans, small businesses can give themselves a better chance of weathering a crisis without suffering major damage. Unfortunately, many SMEs do not have formal crisis management procedures in place. This can lead to chaos and confusion, especially in the early stages of a crisis where precious time and resources can be lost or misdirected during, which can further damage the business (Herbane, 2010b). Spillan and Hough (2003) set out to explore the factors that contribute to small businesses' lack of crisis planning. They surveyed 500 small businesses in the UK and found that only 38% had any kind of formal crisis plan in place. When asked about the importance of having a plan, most respondents said that it was either not important or that they did not know enough about the topic to say. The most common reason given for not having a plan was lack of time, with many respondents saying that they simply did not have the resources to dedicate to planning for something that may never happen. However, the authors note that this lack of planning can have disastrous consequences; when faced with a crisis, businesses without a plan are more likely to shut down permanently.

When confronted with a crisis, SMEs typically adopt various approaches to manage the situation (Herbane, 2013). One study initially identified four common strategies used by SMEs: (1) cutting costs, (2) exploring new revenue streams, (3) intensifying marketing and sales activities, and (4) seeking aid from the government (Burns, 2012). Reducing costs is perhaps the most obvious way for SMEs to deal with a crisis. These responses would strongly depend on the type of crisis that would confront the businesses. By cutting back on expenses, businesses can free up cash flow and make ends meet in the short term. However, cost-cutting measures can also lead to long-term problems if they involve cutting corners on quality or maintenance or compromising customer experience. Diversifying revenue streams is another common strategy for small businesses in crisis mode. By expanding into new markets or offering new products and services, businesses can reduce their dependence on any single income stream. This can provide a much-needed boost during tough times. However, it is important to note that diversification carries its own risks, and small businesses may in the long run not be able to sustain expansion into different areas when not planned for appropriately. Increasing marketing and sales efforts can help bring in additional revenue during a time of upheaval. This could involve anything from offering discounts and promotions to increasing advertising spending. Meanwhile, seeking government assistance can provide much-needed financial support that can help a small business keep its doors open during tough times. The latter option is not always available to all SMEs across different countries.

Naturally, small businesses may respond to crises differently. Another study identified four primary tactics that are frequently employed in such situations: adaptation, avoidance, mitigation, and response (Abdalbaqi, 2021). The most common strategy was adaptation, which involved business owners making changes to their business in order to better deal with the crisis. This could involve anything from changing the service offering or product mix, to altering the way that marketing is done. Avoidance was the second most common strategy, and it involved taking steps to prevent a specific crisis from happening, or prevent the risk from having an impact at all, in the first place. Mitigation was the third most common strategy, and it involved taking steps to reduce the impact of the crisis. This might for example include reducing costs or increasing efficiencies. Response was the least common strategy, and it involved taking direct action to deal with the crisis head on the moment it occurs. This might involve setting up a dedicated crisis response team or working with partners to develop a joint response plan.

There are typically three primary responses among small businesses when faced with a crisis: those who swiftly implement changes to their operations, those who adopt a cautious approach and monitor the situation before taking action, and those who strike a balance between these two strategies (Doern, 2016). Those who immediately start making changes to their businesses typically do so in order to try and reduce the negative impact of the crisis. This could involve anything from changing their products or services to adapting their marketing or business model. For example, a restaurant might start offering delivery or take-out options if dine-in is no longer possible. In contrast, those who take a wait-and-see approach generally do so because they are uncertain about the future and do not want to make any rash decisions, or their current business model is either difficult or costly to adapt. This does not mean that they sit idly by, but rather that they take a more cautious approach, monitoring the situation and only making changes if absolutely necessary. Finally, there are those who adopt a mix of both approaches. This means that they make some changes to their business in order to adapt to a new reality, perhaps temporarily, but also hold off on other changes (e.g. new investment) until a situation becomes clearer.

One of the most important matters for businesses is to maintain communication with stakeholders during a crisis (Herbane, 2013). This includes employees, customers, suppliers, and other key people who have a vested interest in the businesses. Open and honest communication can help to build trust and confidence and prevent misinformation from spreading. Another important strategy is to have a clear action-plan in place for how to deal with a crisis. This should include who is responsible for what, and what the different steps are that need to be taken. Having a plan helps to ensure that everyone knows what they need to do, and know that the response is coordinated and effective.

3 How Do Small Businesses Respond on Natural Crisis?

Natural disasters can have a significant impact on businesses, especially small and medium enterprises (SMEs). In the aftermath of a major disaster, small businesses are often the first to feel the effects. This is due to their location in vulnerable areas, their lack of resources, and their reliance on community infrastructure. This was seen with Cyclone Yasi in North Queensland in 2011, Black Saturday bushfires in Victoria in 2009, Tasmanian bushfires in 2013, Hurricane Katrina in the United States in 2005 and Super Typhoon Haiyan in the Philippines in 2013. In the aftermath of a disaster, SMEs may face a range of challenges including damage to premises, loss of stock, disruptions to supply chains and difficulty accessing finances. While some businesses are able to quickly resume operations, others may take months or even years to recover, if at all. The subsequent examples showcase the various manners in which natural disasters can affect small businesses, along with the ways in which their respective governments provide aid and support to these enterprises:

Cyclone Yasi—North Queensland, 2011: In February 2011, Cyclone Yasi hit north Queensland, causing widespread damage to homes, businesses, and infrastructure. The cyclone caused an estimated $3.6 billion worth of damage and was described as the worst natural disaster in Australia's history. Many SMEs, especially in the tourism industry, were forced to close their doors, while others experienced significant reductions in customer numbers (Mendelson & Carter, 2012). The resulting decline in tourism activity had a knock-on effect on the wider economy, with employment levels also falling. The total number of visitors to the region fell by 11% in the year after the floods and Cyclone Yasi. However, there was considerable variation in the impacts across different types of businesses. For example, while accommodation providers experienced a significant drop in business, tour operators actually saw an increase in bookings (Richardson et al., 2012). This is likely due to the fact that many people were interested in seeing the damage firsthand or wanted to help with relief efforts. For tour operators, catering to curiosity-seekers and to those wishing to do good can be a viable strategy for increasing bookings even in the aftermath of a disaster.

The Queensland Government responded quickly and effectively to the needs of affected communities. The government provided assistance to small businesses affected by the disaster. The government offered various forms of support, including financial aid and counseling services. They established a business recovery hotline and set up temporary office spaces for displaced businesses. Additionally, they created an online portal with information on available resources for affected small businesses. Overall, the Queensland government took significant steps to help small businesses recover from the disaster and get back on their feet. While the Queensland government's response to Yasi was largely successful, there are always lessons to be learned in the wake of this disaster. In particular, the government should continue to work toward improving communication with affected communities and increasing coordination between different agencies (Serrao-Neumann et al., 2018). By doing so, the government can further improve its ability to effectively respond to future natural disasters.

Hurricane Katrina—United States, 2005: In August 2005, Hurricane Katrina hit the US Gulf Coast, causing widespread damage to homes, businesses, and infrastructure. The hurricane resulted in the death of 1833 people and caused an estimated $81 billion worth of damage. Sydnor et al. (2017) conducted a study to assess the degree of damage experienced by small businesses in the New Orleans area. Their analysis showed that approximately one-third of small businesses sustained significant damage, with over half of those businesses being forced to close temporarily. The authors also found that businesses located in low-lying areas or in proximity to levees were more likely to experience damage and disruptions. In the aftermath of the storm, countless small businesses were destroyed or left without power, water, or essential supplies. While some large businesses were able to quickly resume operations, many small businesses were forced to close their doors permanently. In the years following, the number of small businesses in New Orleans declined by nearly 60% (Cater III & Chadwick, 2008).

The federal government's response to Hurricane Katrina was widely criticized, especially in relation to its support for small businesses. The Small Business Administration (SBA) provided nearly $2 billion in loans to business owners in Louisiana and Mississippi. Additionally, the federal government awarded over $1 billion in contracts to small businesses in the region. However the SBA was slow to provide disaster relief loans, and when they did become available, many business owners were unable to qualify. The federal government also failed to provide adequate tax relief for businesses that were impacted by the hurricane (Cater III & Chadwick, 2008).

Super Typhoon Haiyan—Philippines, 2013: In November 2013, Super Typhoon Haiyan hit the Philippines, causing widespread damage to homes, businesses, and infrastructure. The typhoon resulted in the death of 6,300 people and caused an estimated $14 billion worth of damage. In the aftermath of a natural disaster, businesses face a multitude of challenges. For some small businesses, these challenges were exacerbated by the fact that their production facilities were located in an area that was particularly hard hit by Typhoon Haiyan. In a report by Mendoza et al. (2018), it is noted that the typhoon caused significant damage to building and equipment. In addition, many employees were displaced, making it difficult to maintain production levels. For businesses that were able to remain open, trade was significantly impacted as customers stayed away from the affected areas. As a result, many businesses experienced a significant drop in revenue. The Philippine Government provided various forms of assistance to small businesses affected by Super Typhoon Haiyan in 2013. One of the measures implemented was the provision of financial aid and loans through the Department of Trade and Industry, as well as the establishment of a rehabilitation fund for affected businesses. The government also conducted training programs for entrepreneurs on disaster resilience and management, while local governments offered tax relief and waived fees for business permits and licenses to help alleviate the economic impact on small enterprises. Additionally, international organizations such as the World Bank and United Nations Development

Program provided support to small businesses in the form of grants, livelihood assistance, and capacity-building activities.

Tsunami, 2004: The 2004 Indian Ocean tsunami was one of the deadliest natural disasters in history, killing more than 230,000 people and causing devastation across 14 countries. In Sri Lanka, the Galle district was one of the worst-affected areas, with thousands of homes, businesses, and livelihoods destroyed. Over 30,000 people were killed and hundreds of thousands more were left homeless. The tsunami destroyed infrastructure and caused widespread damage to coastal communities. The tsunami also had a significant impact on the tourism industry in Sri Lanka, with many hotels and resorts being destroyed or badly damaged (Wickramasinghe & Takano, 2007). In the immediate aftermath of the tsunami, tourist numbers fell sharply, as frightened travelers canceled their plans to visit Sri Lanka. The Sri Lankan government struggled to provide relief and support to those affected (Dasanayaka et al., 2020). This included low-interest loans and grants, which helped many small business owners rebuild their shops and factories. In addition, the government also waived certain taxes and fees for affected businesses, further easing their financial burden. Another important step taken by the government was to provide training and support for affected business owners. This included workshops on disaster preparedness and business management, as well as counseling services for those dealing with trauma or other mental health issues.

The Northridge earthquake-USA, 1994: The Northridge earthquake-USA, 1994 was one of the most destructive earthquakes to hit California in recent memory. The 6.7 magnitude quake struck at 4:31 am on January 17th, 1994 and caused widespread damage across Los Angeles and the surrounding counties. In addition to the physical damage caused by the quake, businesses also suffered significant financial losses due to disrupted supply chains and lost customers. One of the biggest challenges faced by businesses after the Northridge earthquake was rebuilding damaged infrastructure. Many businesses lost their office space or warehouses in the quake, and had to start from scratch in terms of finding new locations. In addition, many businesses also had to deal with damaged inventory and equipment. Another challenge faced by businesses was dealing with the loss of customers. Many people who lived in areas affected by the quake were displaced and moved to other parts of the state or country. This led to a decrease in customer base for many businesses, which made it difficult for them to generate revenue. The Small Business Administration (SBA) Disaster Assistance program provided critical support to affected small businesses. The SBA helped business owners with loan programs and counseling services. Additionally, the agency worked with local government and private organizations to provide resources and assistance.

From a business perspective SMEs often experience the most lasting impacting effects of any type of natural disaster. These businesses not only suffer damage to their physical infrastructure, but they also face lost revenue as well as disruptions in supply chains due to these events happening so close together. Especially what cash-flows are tight and with fewer reserves to fall back on many SMEs struggle. Yet even with all these challenges standing before them, there is hope for SMEs who have managed through times where things were tough before by building up social capital. Businesses with social networks can help each other out in the wake of natural disasters.

4   Social Capital as a Resource for Managing Crisis

The basic idea of social capital theory is that humans are social animals and that our success in life depends heavily on the networks we form with other people. Social capital has been defined in numerous ways, but at its core, it refers to the networks of relationships and resources that people can draw upon to achieve their goals. Pierre Bourdieu (1985) was a French sociologist who is best known for his theory of social capital. Social capital is generated when individuals interact with each other in social space. This interaction gives rise to bonds of trust and reciprocity, which are the basis for cooperation and collective action. As some have explained it, social capital is a unique resource that often increases as you use it, as using it further builds bonds, generates trust, and expands networks. While social capital is a resource, Bourdieu argued that it could also be a source of inequality. While some people have extensive networks of relationships and resources, others do not. This unequal distribution of social capital means that those with more social capital have greater advantages in life than those with less social capital. Bourdieu's theory of social capital has been used widely, from why some people are more successful than others are, to why some countries are more developed than others are.

While social capital can be a source of power and advantage, it can also be a source of conflict and inequality. Bourdieu's theory of social capital can help us to understand the complex ways in which social relationships and resources are distributed in society. For example, scholars have used Bourdieu's concepts to study the development of cooperative relationships within organizations, the formation of political parties, and the dynamics of economic development. Putnam (1993) then describes how social capital can be created and strengthened through activities such as voting, volunteering, and participating in community organizations. Similar to Coleman (1990) suggests that social capital is created when people develop relationships of trust and reciprocity. These relationships allow individuals to pool resources and cooperate toward shared goals. As a result, social capital can lead to improved outcomes for individuals and communities. Bourdieu, Coleman, and Putnam each have their own distinct theories when it comes to social capital. However, they all largely agree that social capital is integral for a functioning society. In Bourdieu's theory, social capital is a form of economic and cultural capital (Tzanakis, 2013). Coleman believed that social capital is what allows members of a society to cooperate effectively. Putnam's conception of social capital is similar to Coleman's in that he also emphasizes the importance of cooperation among members of a society. However, he adds that social capital also includes "the extent to which members of a community trust and help one another" (Tzanakis, 2013, p. 6).

In an article by Szreter and Woolcock (2004) they discuss the concept of social capital and its potential implications for public health. The authors argue that social capital has three main components: bonding, bridging, and linking. Bonding refers to the strong ties that bind people together within a close-knit community. These ties can take many forms, including kinship bonds, shared ethnic or religious identity, or simply shared life experiences. Bridging social capital, on the other hand, consists of weaker ties that link people across different groups. These ties can help to build understanding and cooperation between different groups, and can be an important source of information and support. Finally, linking social capital refers to the links between individuals and institutions (such as government or business). These links can help individuals to access resources and opportunities that they would not be able to access on their own. Each type of social capital can contribute to the economic development of a community by facilitating cooperation, innovation, and knowledge sharing. In addition, social capital can also promote social cohesion and inclusion, which can lead to better health outcomes and increased civic engagement. Therefore, social capital is an important asset for any community interested in promoting economic and social development.

From a social capital theory perspective, the response of small businesses to Super Typhoon Haiyan in the Philippines in 2013 can be analyzed in terms of their access to and utilization of social networks and resources. One example of a small business that was able to respond effectively to the typhoon through its social capital is the microfinance organization Alalay sa Kaunlaran (ASKI). ASKI had established strong relationships with its clients prior to the disaster, which allowed it to quickly mobilize resources and support for those affected by the typhoon. Through its network of branches across affected areas, ASKI was able to distribute relief goods and provide financial assistance to clients who lost their homes or livelihoods. Another example is that of Jollibee Foods Corporation, a popular fast food chain in the Philippines. Despite sustaining significant damage to several of its stores during the typhoon, Jollibee was able to quickly reopen many locations due in part to its strong relationships with suppliers and contractors. By leveraging these relationships, Jollibee was able to secure necessary repairs and supplies more quickly than some other businesses. In the case of small businesses responding to the 2004 Tsunami, one example is the story of a group of women entrepreneurs in Sri Lanka who banded together to form a cooperative after the tsunami destroyed their individual businesses. By pooling their resources and working together, they were able to secure loans and rebuild their businesses more quickly than they would have been able to on their own.

4.1 Cognitive Social Capital

When it comes to social capital, there are three main types: structural, cognitive, and relational (Nahapiet & Ghoshal, 1998). Each type of social capital has its own unique benefits, but cognitive social capital is often seen as the most important for small businesses. Structural social capital refers to the resources that are available within a community or network. This could include things like financial resources, knowledge, or even physical resources. Structural social capital is important because it can provide small businesses with the resources they need to get started and grow. Relational social capital refers to the relationships between people within a community or network. These relationships can be beneficial because they can help people connect with each other and exchange information. Relational social capital is often seen as less important than structural social capital, but it can still be beneficial for small businesses. Cognitive social capital refers to the shared beliefs and values within a community or network. This type of social capital is important because it can help people trust and cooperate with each other. Cognitive social capital is often seen as the most important type of social capital for small businesses (Lee & Jones, 2008).

There are many reasons why cognitive social capital is seen as the most important type of social capital for small businesses. One reason is that cognitive social capital can help small businesses build trust with their customers. Trust is an important part of any business relationship, and it can be difficult to establish without cognitive social capital. Another reason why cognitive social capital is so important is that it can help small businesses cooperate with each other. Cooperation is essential for any business, and it can be difficult to achieve without cognitive social capital.

Cognitive social capital is also important because it can help small businesses connect with their customers. Customers are often more likely to do business with companies that they feel connected to. Additionally, cognitive social capital can help small businesses build relationships with their suppliers. Strong relationships with suppliers can lead to better prices and terms, which can benefit small businesses. While cognitive social capital is a relatively new concept, it has already made a significant impact on the field of entrepreneurship. By providing a more nuanced understanding of how entrepreneurs learn and develop new ideas, it has helped to improve the success rate of new businesses. In addition, by focusing on the quality of relationships and networks, rather than the quantity, it has also helped to create more diverse and inclusive ecosystems for entrepreneurship. For example, after Hurricane Katrina in New Orleans, many small business owners drew on shared cultural values such as hospitality and resilience to guide their response efforts. Some entrepreneurs opened up their homes or businesses to serve as shelters for displaced residents, while others worked together to clean up debris and rebuild damaged infrastructure. By acting in accordance with these shared beliefs and values, these small businesses were able to build trust with their customers and communities while also contributing to the broader recovery effort.

There are many benefits of cognitive social capital, but there are also some potential drawbacks. One potential drawback is that cognitive social capital can sometimes lead to conflict within a community or network. Conflict can be beneficial if it leads to positive change, but it can also be detrimental if it causes division. Additionally, cognitive social capital can sometimes lead to a false sense of security. This false sense of security can cause people to take risks that they would not normally take, which can lead to problems. Despite the potential drawbacks, cognitive social capital is still seen as the most important type of social capital for small businesses. This is because cognitive social capital can provide small businesses with trust, cooperation, and connections with their customers and suppliers. These things are essential for any business, and they can be difficult to achieve without cognitive social capital.

4.2   Accessing Social Capital for Small Businesses

Small businesses can access social capital by getting involved in ***civic engagement*** and being ***socially responsible*** citizens in their ***local communities***. Community involvement helps businesses build trust and credibility, which can lead to more customers and clients. Additionally, by being good corporate citizens, businesses can create a positive image for themselves, which can attract more customers and investors.

Civic engagement: Community involvement is a key way for businesses to accessed social capital. By getting involved in civic activities and causes, businesses can show they care about more than just profits. This helps build trust and credibility with potential customers and the community at large. Additionally, civic engagement can help businesses make connections with other business owners and leaders. These connections can be helpful in finding new customers, suppliers, or partners.

Social responsibility: Another way businesses can access social capital is by being socially responsible citizens in their communities. This means more than just donating money to charitable causes; it also includes things like volunteering, supporting local events, and being environmentally conscious. By doing these things, businesses can show they are committed to making a positive impact on the world around them. This can attract more customers and investors who want to support companies that are doing good. Additionally, social responsibility can help businesses build stronger relationships with employees, clients, and customers.

Local community: Finally, businesses can access social capital by being active members of their communities. This means getting involved in local civic groups and organizations, attending community events, and networking with other business owners. Community involvement helps businesses build trust and credibility, which can lead to more customers and clients. Additionally, by being involved in the community, businesses can learn about the needs and wants of their potential customers. This knowledge can help them better serve their target market and grow their business.

Small businesses play a crucial role in their local communities, and during times of crises, their involvement in civic engagement and social responsibility becomes even more important. By actively participating in community initiatives and supporting local causes, small businesses can help build a sense of solidarity and resilience among residents. This can be achieved through donations, volunteering, or simply by raising awareness about important issues. Additionally, small businesses that prioritize social responsibility are often viewed as trustworthy and reliable by their customers. As such, they are better positioned to weather economic downturns or other crises that may impact their business operations. Overall, the involvement of small businesses in civic engagement and social responsibility is not only beneficial for the community but also for the long-term success of the business itself.

5 Small Businesses' Business Continuity Management

In the event of a natural disaster or other crisis, small businesses can use business continuity management (BCM) to help cope with the situation. Business continuity management is a framework that helps organizations ensure that they are prepared for, and can respond to, disruptions. It includes planning for how to keep operations running during and after a crisis, as well as how to recover quickly. Business Continuity Management finds it roots in Disaster Recovery Planning. Disaster Recovery Planning was first introduced in the 1960s, in response to the increasing frequency and impact of natural disasters. Disaster recovery planning became increasingly formalized in the 1970s and 1980s, as businesses realized the importance of being able to recover from a disaster with minimal disruption to operations. One of the first documented cases of a company planning for disruptions to its business comes from the 1800s, when Levi Strauss & Co. created a contingency plan in case its San Francisco headquarters were destroyed by an earthquake.

In the 1990s, disaster recovery planning evolved into business continuity planning, as organizations began to recognize the need to protect not just their physical infrastructure, but also their people and processes. Business continuity planning is now recognized as a vital part of any organization's risk management strategy. The International Organization for Standardization (ISO) published the first international standard for business continuity management in 2006. This standard, ISO 22301, provides a framework for organizations to plan, implement, and maintain an effective business continuity management system. ISO 22301 is based on the disaster recovery planning standards developed by the British Standards Institution (BSI), which were first published in 1992. The BSI standards were subsequently adopted by the International Standards Organization (ISO) in 1999.

Today, business continuity management is recognized as a vital part of any organization's risk management strategy. It helps organizations to protect their people, processes, and infrastructure from the impact of disruptions, whether they are caused by natural disasters, human error, or malicious attacks. Business continuity management is an essential element of organizational resilience.

The development of business continuity management has been shaped by three main factors: natural disasters, social capital, and community (Herbane, 2010a). Natural disasters have been a major driver of change in business continuity management, forcing businesses to adapt their practices to cope with the increasing frequency and severity of natural disasters. Social capital has also played a role in the development of business continuity management, with businesses investing in community-based resilience initiatives to build up their social capital. Finally, community interactions have been an important factor in shaping business continuity management practices, with businesses sharing information and best practices to improve their chance of surviving a crisis.

5.1 Strategizing Business Continuity Planning

A business continuity planning strategy is a plan that outlines how a business will continue to operate during and after an emergency or disruptions. The goal of a business continuity planning strategy is to keep the business running, minimize downtime, and protect employees, customers, and other stakeholders. There are many potential hazards that could disrupt business operations, so it is important to have a plan in place to address each type of scenario. Common disruptions include natural disasters, power outages, IT failures, and pandemics. Depending on the size and complexity of the organization, a business continuity planning strategy can be as simple as having an emergency backup plan for key personnel and systems. For larger organizations, a business continuity planning strategy may be more comprehensive and include disaster recovery plans, incident response plans, and business continuity plans. The key to a successful business continuity planning strategy is to identify the potential risks to the business and develop plans to address them. The plan should be reviewed and updated on a regular basis to ensure it remains current.

There are many benefits to having a business continuity planning strategy in place. A well-developed business continuity planning can help minimize downtime, protect employees and customers, safeguard critical business operations, and improve the organization's overall resilience. In addition, a business continuity planning can help an organization to meet its regulatory and compliance obligations. Many industries have specific requirements for business continuity planning, so a business continuity planning can help an organization to stay compliant with these regulations. Finally, a business continuity planning can also provide peace of mind for businesses and their stakeholders. Knowing that there is a plan in place to address potential disruptions can help to reduce anxiety and stress in the event of an emergency.

There are several steps involved in developing a business continuity planning strategy. The first step is to assess the risks to the business. This includes identifying potential hazards, assessing the likelihood of them occurring, and estimating the impact they would have on the business. The next step is to develop plans to address the risks. This may include plans for alternative work locations, backup systems, and communication protocols. The key is to ensure that the plans are comprehensive and cover all potential scenarios. The third step is to test the plans, which helps to ensure that they are effective and that all employees know what to do in the event of an emergency. Testing can be done through simulations, tabletop exercises, or full-scale drills. Finally, the fourth step is to maintain and update the plan on a regular basis. As business operations change, so too should the business continuity planning. Regular updates help to ensure that the plan remains current and relevant.

5.2 Pitfalls in Developing a Business Continuity Planning Strategy

There are several common mistakes that can be made when developing a business continuity planning strategy. One mistake is to neglect the importance of assessing *all* potential risks to the business. This step is critical to identify potential hazards and develop plans to address them. A second mistake is to fail to involve all stakeholders in the process. A business continuity planning strategy affects everyone in the organization, so it's important to get input from all employees, customers, and other stakeholders. Stakeholder involvement is also important to have more diverse views toward solutions, as sometimes different employees from different departments can add innovative solutions to potential problems, and by testing (through simulation e.g.,) the solutions with all the stakeholders, obvious mistakes can be identified that might be overlooked if a stakeholder with specific expertise is overlooked. A third mistake is to develop a plan that is too narrowly focused. The goal of a business continuity planning is to keep the business running in any event, so the plan should be comprehensive and cover a wide range of potential scenarios. Finally, a fourth mistake is to fail to test the plan. Testing is essential to ensure that the plan is effective and that employees know what to do in the event of an emergency. As well as stated above, testing can remove initial flaws from drafted plans.

6 Conclusion

Small businesses are among the most vulnerable during times of crisis. A major disruption can quickly threaten their very existence. Therefore it is important for small businesses to have a plan in place to deal with crises, and one of the key components of any effective plan, as demonstrated in the chapter past, is social capital. Social capital is the networks and relationships that businesses rely on to function. It includes things like community relationships, supplier relationships, customer loyalty, and employee expertise. During a crisis, these relationships can be essential in helping a small business weather the storm. They can provide access to resources, information, and support that may not be available otherwise. In the small business context, social capital and business continuity management are often seen as complementary approaches to crisis management. Social capital can provide the networks and resources that are needed to effectively respond to a crisis, while business continuity management can help to ensure that essential operations can continue. By taking steps to build strong social capital and implementing a comprehensive business continuity management program, small businesses can increase their chances of surviving and thriving during even the most challenging times.

References

Abdalbaqi, A. M. S. (2021). *A qualitative study for crisis management strategies used by small business leaders.* (Doctoral dissertation), Concordia University Chicago.

Bourdieu, P. (1985). The social space and the genesis of groups. *Social Science Information, 24*(2), 195–220.

Breier, M., Kallmuenzer, A., Clauss, T., Gast, J., Kraus, S., & Tiberius, V. (2021). The role of business model innovation in the hospitality industry during the COVID-19 crisis. *International Journal of Hospitality Management, 92*, 102723.

Burns, K. F. (2012). *Assessing and exploring strategic crisis management planning in michigan small businesses.* (Doctoral dissertation), Lawrence Technological University.

Cater, J. J., III, & Chadwick, K. (2008). Response to Hurricane Katrina: A small business approach. *Academy of Strategic Management Journal, 7*, 55.

Coleman, J. S. (1990). *The foundations of social theory.* Harvard University Press.

Corey, C. M., & Deitch, E. A. (2011). Factors affecting business recovery immediately after Hurricane Katrina. *Journal of Contingencies and Crisis Management, 19*(3), 169–181.

Dasanayaka, S. W. S. B., Jayarathna, W., Serhan, O. A., & Gleason, K. (2020). Recovery from natural disaster: A study on tsunami-affected micro, small and medium enterprises in Galle and Matara districts in Sri Lanka. *International Journal of Risk Assessment and Management, 23*(2), 149–168.

Doern, R. (2016). Entrepreneurship and crisis management: The experiences of small businesses during the London 2011 riots. *International Small Business Journal, 34*(3), 276–302. https://doi.org/10.1177/0266242614553863

Doern, R., Williams, N., & Vorley, T. (2019). Special issue on entrepreneurship and crises: Business as usual? An introduction and review of the literature. *Entrepreneurship & Regional Development, 31*(5–6), 400–412.

Herbane, B. (2010a). The evolution of business continuity management: A historical review of practices and drivers. *Business History, 52*(6), 978–1002.

Herbane, B. (2010b). Small business research: Time for a crisis-based view. *International Small Business Journal, 28*(1), 43–64.

Herbane, B. (2013). Exploring crisis management in UK small-and medium-sized enterprises. *Journal of Contingencies and Crisis Management, 21*(2), 82–95.

Lee, R., & Jones, O. (2008). Networks, communication and learning during business start-up: The creation of cognitive social capital. *International Small Business Journal, 26*(5), 559–594.

Mendelson, D., & Carter, R. (2012). Catastrophic loss and the law: A comparison between 2009 Victorian Black Saturday fires and 2011 Queensland floods and Cyclone Yasi. *University of Tasmania Law Review, 31*(2), 32–54.

Mendoza, R. U., Lau, A., & Castillejos, M. T. Y. (2018). Can SMEs survive natural disasters? Eva Marie arts and crafts versus typhoon Yolanda. *International Journal of Disaster Risk Reduction, 31*, 938–952.

Nahapiet, J., & Ghoshal, S. (1998). Social capital, intellectual capital, and the organizational advantage. *Academy of Management Review, 23*(2), 242–266.

Nguyen, H., & Sawang, S. (2016). Juggling or struggling? Work and family interface and its buffers among small business owners. *Entrepreneurship Research Journal, 6*(2), 207–246.

Putnam, R. (1993). The prosperous community: Social capital and public life. *The American Prospect, 13*(4), 35–42.

Richardson, S., March, R., Lewis, J., & Radel, K. (2012). Analysing the impact of the 2011 natural disasters on the Central Queensland tourism industry. *TEAM Journal of Hospitality and Tourism, 9*(1), 1–14.

Sawang, S., O'Connor, P. J., Kivits, R. A., & Jones, P. (2020). Business owner-managers' job autonomy and job satisfaction: Up, down or no change? *Frontiers in Psychology, 11*, 1506.

Serrao-Neumann, S., Crick, F., & Low Choy, D. (2018). Post-disaster social recovery: Disaster governance lessons learnt from Tropical Cyclone Yasi. *Natural Hazards, 93*(3), 1163–1180.

Spillan, J., & Hough, M. (2003). Crisis planning in small businesses: Importance, impetus and indifference. *European Management Journal, 21*(3), 398–407.

Sydnor, S., Niehm, L., Lee, Y., Marshall, M., & Schrank, H. (2017). Analysis of post-disaster damage and disruptive impacts on the operating status of small businesses after Hurricane Katrina. *Natural Hazards, 85*(3), 1637–1663.

Szreter, S., & Woolcock, M. (2004). Health by association? Social capital, social theory, and the political economy of public health. *International Journal of Epidemiology, 33*(4), 650–667.

Tzanakis, M. (2013). Social capital in Bourdieu's, Coleman's and Putnam's theory: Empirical evidence and emergent measurement issues. *Educate, 13*(2), 2–23.

Weick, K. E. (1995). *Sensemaking in organizations* (Vol. 3). Sage.

Wickramasinghe, V., & Takano, S.-E. (2007). Revival of tourism in Sri Lanka following the December 2004 Indian Ocean tsunami. *Journal of Natural Disaster Science, 29*(2), 83–95.

3

COVID-19 and Small Businesses Responses

Abstract The period roughly from 2020 and well into 2022 has been one of the most challenging for small businesses around the world. The COVID-19 pandemic has had a significant impact on many businesses, with some having to close their doors temporarily and others struggling to keep afloat. COVID-19 has demonstrated how unpredictable and impactful a crisis can be. It has also demonstrated how unpredictable societal response to a crisis can be. While the pandemic is now largely behind us, with several vaccines developed, countries around the world are taking measures to help prevent further outbreaks of the virus. The outbreak of COVID-19 has had a significant impact on the world, both in terms of mental and physical health as well as economically. The pandemic has also seen a shift in consumer behavior, with people becoming more cautious about spending their money and a large shift to online consumption. This has put increased pressure on small businesses who have had to adjust their operations to stay competitive. This chapter illustrates to what extent COVID-19 impacted on small businesses and how these business cope with the situation, especially post pandemic, and what lessons can be learned from these experiences.

Keywords Crisis impacts • COVID-19 • Small business crisis response • Crisis coping

1 COVID-19 Impact on Small Businesses

The early impacts of the COVID-19 pandemic were devastating for small businesses across the globe. Sales plummeted, and many businesses were struggling to stay afloat. The pandemic has had a significant negative impact on sales, with businesses of all sizes seeing declines. The most affected businesses are those that rely heavily on footfall and face-to-face interactions, such as restaurants, retail stores and hairdressers and beauty salons. These businesses have seen comparative sales drop over the year by over 60% in some cases (Fairlie & Fossen, 2022). Other businesses, such as manufacturing and construction, have also been impacted, but to a lesser extent as in some cases, work could continue, albeit under restrictions. Overall, it is fair to say that the pandemic has had a widespread negative impact on business sales (Fairlie & Fossen, 2022). Revenue at small businesses has collapsed in the early stages of the pandemic, due to lockdown disruptions in supply chains and customer demand, as well as increased costs associated with health and safety measures (Buffington et al., 2020). Many business owners were forced to consume their savings just to keep their businesses afloat (Kim et al., 2020).

Another visible effect of the pandemic has been a sharp increase in layoffs and unemployment. The number of small businesses that have laid off workers since the start of the pandemic is nearly double the number that did so during the recession of 2007–2009 (Bartik et al., 2020). Businesses that have been forced to close due to shutdown orders were not surprisingly more likely to lay off workers than those that remained open. Although the total number of layoffs is currently lower than that of the 2007-2008 recession, the rate at which they have taken place during the COVID-19 pandemic has been significantly faster. In fact, more than half of all job cuts occurred within the first two months of the outbreak (Bartik et al., 2020). The sharp increase in unemployment will likely have long lasting effects on society, including increased poverty and homelessness, as well as mental health problems and crime. Businesses which classified as financially fragile before the pandemic hit were found to be more likely to go out of business entirely, and their employees more likely to lose their jobs as a result. Data from the study showed that these businesses were less likely to survive the pandemic than those which were not struggling financially beforehand, underlining the need for policy interventions which specifically target small businesses most vulnerable to failure during such crises (Bartik et al., 2020).

Further, the pandemic has led to a decrease in the number of new business startups, as well as a decrease in the growth rate of existing small businesses. In addition, the pandemic has also caused an increase in business closures among small businesses (Belitski et al., 2022). The pandemic has made it difficult for small businesses to obtain loans and other forms of financing. This has further exacerbated the financial challenges faced by small businesses during the pandemic. That is why it is so important for small businesses to have the ability to bounce back from adversity. Psychological resilience is a critical factor in determining whether small businesses will survive and thrive in the face of challenging circumstances.

2 Small Businesses Resilience

Psychological resilience is a topic of interest to many disciplines, including psychology, sociology, and anthropology. It has been defined in various ways, but generally, it refers to the ability to bounce back from stressful or difficult situations. It is a key component of mental health, and it is something that can be developed and strengthened over time (Fletcher & Sarkar, 2013). For example, a recent study found that military personnel who were more resilient had lower levels of post-traumatic stress disorder (PTSD) symptoms after returning from deployment overseas (Lee et al., 2013). Psychological resilience is a concept with a long history, but it has only recently been the focus of scientific research. As our understanding of this concept grows, it has the potential to improve our ability to prevent and cope with mental health problems.

It is widely accepted that both business and psychological resilience are important in today's world. But what is the difference between the two? Business resilience is about being able to withstand and recover from disruptions to your business, whether they are caused by external factors like natural disasters or internal factors like financial difficulties (Adekola

& Clelland, 2020). Psychological resilience, on the other hand, is about bouncing back from difficult life events or challenges (Chadwick & Raver, 2020). Both business and psychological resilience are important for coping with stress and adversity. However, there are some key differences between the two. Businesses need to be able to quickly adapt to changing circumstances and continue operating despite setbacks, whereas individuals need to be able to cope with personal stressors and challenges without letting them overwhelm them. Businesses also need to have robust plans in place for dealing with disruptions, whereas individuals can often rely on their own personal resources and coping mechanisms. There are many similarities between business and psychological resilience, but there are also some important differences. Both are essential for dealing with stress and adversity, but they serve different purposes. Businesses need to be able to quickly adapt and continue operating despite setbacks, while individuals need to be able to cope with personal stressors without letting them overwhelm them.

There are two different ways to define business resilience: definitions that include only "after-event" components and definitions that contain both "before" and "after-event" components (Carlson et al., 2012). The former type of definition typically focuses on a company's ability to recover from a disruptive event. This might include factors such as having a robust emergency response plan, being able to quickly resume operations after an interruption, and having insurance in place to cover the costs of repairs or replacement. The latter type of definition takes a broader view of business resilience, encompassing both the ability to withstand a potentially damaging event and the ability to bounce back quickly afterwards. This would involve factors such as having a diversified supply chain, having a good reputation with customers, and having a strong financial position. Both types of definitions have their merits, but the latter is generally considered to be more comprehensive. This is because it recognizes that a company's ability to survive and thrive in the face of adversity goes beyond simply being able to recover from an event. It also considers the importance of being prepared for an event in the first place, and of having the resources and support in place to make a speedy recovery afterwards.

Business resilience and community resilience are two important concepts that are often used interchangeably. However, there are some important distinctions between the two. Business resilience refers to a business' ability to withstand and recover from disruptions (Adekola & Clelland, 2020). This includes everything from weather-related events to political upheaval. Community resilience, on the other hand, refers to a community's ability to maintain its social cohesion and functioning in the face of adversity (Adekola & Clelland, 2020). This can be everything from economic downturns to natural disasters. There are some key similarities between business resilience and community resilience. Both involve a community's ability to maintain its operations in the face of adversity. Both also require a community to have some level of preparedness for disruptions. However, there are also some important differences. Business resilience is more focused on a business' ability to recover from disruptions, while community resilience is more focused on a community's ability to maintain its social cohesion and functioning. Business resilience is also typically more short-term in nature, while community resilience is more long-term. Ultimately, business resilience and community resilience are two sides of the same coin (Adekola & Clelland, 2020). Both involve a community's ability to withstand and recover from adversity. However, there are some important distinctions between the two concepts. Understanding these distinctions is essential for effectively addressing the challenges that communities face.

Among small businesses, family businesses tend to be more resilient than non-family businesses (Amann & Jaussaud, 2012). There are a number of reasons why family businesses are thought to be more resilient. Firstly, family businesses tend to have a longer-term perspective than their non-family counterparts do. This is because families are often looking to hand the business down to future generations, so they take a long-term view of things. Secondly, family businesses tend to be more conservative in their approach to risk. They are often less likely to take on debt and they tend to reinvest profits back into the business. This gives them a strong financial foundation which helps them weather tough times. Thirdly, family businesses often have very strong ties to their communities. They are often the biggest employer in a town or region, so they have a vested interest in making sure that the community does well. This can help them weather economic downturns, as people are more likely to support a local business than one that is based elsewhere. Finally, family businesses often have very strong relationships with their employees. Because employees are often treated more like family members than just workers, they tend to be more loyal and committed to the business. This can make it easier for a family business to weather tough times, as employees are less likely to leave during difficult periods.

Family businesses are more likely to display what they call a "culture of crisis" which is characterized by a focused effort to maintain business operations despite difficult circumstances (Amann & Jaussaud, 2012). In contrast, non-family businesses are more likely to experience what the authors call a "culture of decline" which is characterized by a more passive response to the economic downturn (Amann & Jaussaud, 2012). While non-family businesses may be more concerned with short-term profit margins, family businesses may place a higher priority on long-term sustainability. As a result, family businesses may be more likely to weather an economic downturn, even if it means making sacrifices in the short-term. They tend to have a longer-term perspective, which means they are less likely to make short-term decisions that could jeopardize the future of the business. They also tend to be more conservative in their approach to risk, which helps them weather tough times. And finally, their strong ties to their employees and communities help them weather difficult periods (Beech et al., 2019).

According to a systematic literature review (Korber & McNaughton, 2017), resilient small business owner-managers are more likely to persevere in the face of adversity and to bounce back quickly from setbacks. Further, they find that resilient small business owner-managers are more likely to be proactive in their approach to business challenges and opportunities. Resilient small business owner-managers are also more likely to have a positive impact on their employees and organizations. These findings provide valuable insights into the role of resilience in entrepreneurship. The article defines resilience as "the ability of individuals to spring back or recover quickly from difficult situations" (Korber & McNaughton, 2017, p. 1129). In other words, it is the ability to persevere in the face of adversity. On the other hand, entrepreneurship is described as "the process of designing, launching, and running a new business or enterprise"

(Korber & McNaughton, 2017, p. 1129). In other words, it is the act of turning an innovative idea into a reality. The authors note that both resilience and entrepreneurship are important individual traits that can help contribute to success in business. According to their statement, "an entrepreneurial mindset characterized by optimism, self-efficacy, and internal locus of control has been found to positively moderate the effect of stress on business performance" (Korber & McNaughton, 2017, p. 1141). In other words, a resilient and entrepreneurial mindset can help small business owner-managers overcome stress and achieve success in business. Businesses led by small business owner-managers who are psychologically resilient are more likely to survive in the early stages of development (Chadwick & Raver, 2020). This is likely due to the fact that resilient small business owner-managers are better able to cope with stress and setbacks, and they are also more likely to persist in the face of adversity. In addition, psychological resilience is associated with higher levels of innovation and creativity, which are essential for success in the highly competitive world of new venture creation (Chadwick & Raver, 2020).

3 Factors Contribute to Small Business Resilience

The COVID-19 pandemic has presented small businesses with unforeseen difficulties. While some have had to shut down permanently, others have faced challenges adapting to the new reality. However, there are still some businesses that have managed to withstand the storm and even flourish in the "new normal." There are several factors that can contribute to small business resilience in the face of adversity. One key factor is diversification, which involves expanding a business's product line or services offered to reduce reliance on a single area of the business. Another important factor is having adequate financial resources, including cash reserves and access to credit, which can help small businesses weather unexpected disruptions. Business agility competency is also crucial for resilience, as it allows companies to quickly adapt and respond to changes in the market environment. Additionally, government support can provide small businesses with critical resources during times of crisis, such as funding assistance and regulatory flexibility. Finally, entrepreneurial well-being—including the mental and emotional health of small business owners—is an essential factor in their ability to navigate difficult circumstances. By prioritizing these factors, small businesses can increase their resilience and better withstand unexpected challenges. This section will explore the primary factors that contribute to small business resilience, including diversification, financial resources, business agility competency, government support, and entrepreneurial well-being.

3.1 Diversification

Customer-country diversification can help firms to deal with inventory disruptions during periods of economic uncertainty, such as the COVID-19 pandemic (Ke et al., 2022). Comparing the manufacturing sector in the pre-pandemic period (2003–2018) with the period during and immediately after the pandemic (January–July 2020), firms with a more diversified customer base were better able to maintain inventory efficiency during the pandemic, as they were less likely to experience disruptions in demand from any one country (Ke et al., 2022). The authors suggest that firms should therefore consider diversifying their customer base as a way to mitigating the risks of disruptive events. This is particularly important for firms that operate in industries with long supply chains and high levels of inventory, such as the manufacturing sector.

Diversification is a business strategy that can help organizations weather the storm of an economic downturn, as it allows them to spread their risk across multiple products and markets. There are a few different ways that small businesses can go about diversifying. One option is to offer a variety of similar products or services. For example, a small business that specializes in selling one type of product could start carrying a related line of products. This way, even if sales of the original product decline, the business will still have other revenue streams to fall back on. Another option is to offer different types of products or services altogether. This can be a riskier strategy, but it can also pay off in a big way if done correctly. For example, a small business that has always sold products could start offering services instead. Or, a business that has always served a local market could start selling online or expanding to other areas. The benefits of diversification are twofold. First, it helps to reduce risk by spreading out your bets across different markets and products. This way, if one market or product line fails, you have others to fall back on. Second, diversification can also lead to economies of scale, as you can leverage your existing infrastructure and knowledge base to expand into new areas. A number of small businesses use diversification to cope with COVID-19. For example, small retail businesses open an online store to reach new customers. Manufacturers start selling their products directly to consumers instead of relying on retailers. Restaurants start offering delivery or takeout service. Clothing companies start selling face masks or other items that people need during the pandemic.

3.2 Financial Resources

Financial resources are also a key factor in supporting small businesses during periods of shocks and stress. Businesses with access to financial resources are more likely to be resilient in the face of disruptions than those without such resources (Eggers, 2020). During the COVID-19 pandemic, many small businesses found themselves struggling to stay afloat. However, those with strong financial resources were better equipped to weather the storm. For example, businesses with cash reserves were able to cover expenses when revenue declined, while those with access to credit could secure additional funding to keep their operations running. Additionally, businesses that had diversified their revenue streams or offered online sales channels were often more resilient than those that relied solely on in-person sales. By leveraging their financial resources and adapting their business models as needed, these companies were able to navigate the challenges of the pandemic and emerge stronger on the other side.

To strengthen their financial resources and increase resilience, small businesses can take several steps. First and foremost, it is important to establish a cash reserve—ideally enough to cover at least three months of expenses—that can be drawn upon during times of crisis. Businesses should also explore options for securing credit lines or loans that can provide additional funding if needed. Additionally, diversifying revenue streams through new product offerings or online sales channels can help mitigate risk and ensure a steady stream of income even during challenging times. Finally, businesses should regularly review their financial statements and projections to identify potential risks and opportunities for improvement. By taking proactive steps to strengthen their financial resources, small businesses can enhance their resilience and position themselves for long-term success.

3.3 Business Agility Competency

Business agility can help small businesses create resiliency in the face of crisis. Business agility competency is a term used to describe the ability of an organization to rapidly adapt to changes in the business environment (Troise et al., 2022). This includes the ability to respond quickly to customer demands, market trends, and new technology. Agility is a key competency for organizations of all sizes, but it is especially important for small businesses as they typically have fewer resources than larger organizations. The implications of agility can be seen in many studies, such as Chan et al. (2019) investigated the role of agility in responding to disruptive digital innovation, using a case study of a small business context. The results showed that agility is a key success factor in small businesses' ability to respond quickly and effectively to disruptive innovation. The study also found that agility enables firms to tap into new markets and create new value propositions. Therefore, they must be able to make changes quickly in order to compete effectively. Arbussa et al. (2017) explored the role of agility in business model renewal. Their work demonstrated that a company must have strategic agility in order to be successful. This means being able to quickly adapt to changes in the marketplace and make decisions that are responsive to those changes.

Business agility has become an essential characteristic of successful business in the global economy. The ability to rapidly adapt to changing markets, technologies, and customer needs is critical for firms seeking to maintain a competitive edge. However, agility is not just about being able to act quickly; it also requires a deep understanding of the relationships between different business functions and the ability to orchestrate them in a way that maximizes value. This is where the work by Nyamrunda and Freeman (2021) on dynamic relational capability comes in. Their study of small and medium-sized enterprises in transitional economies highlights the importance of trust as a key driver of agility. Firms that are able to build trust-based relationships with their employees, suppliers, and customers are better able to respond quickly and effectively to change. Business agility (market, technology, and business model) can be enhanced by judicious use of network resources (Liu & Yang, 2020). For example, regarding market orientation, small and medium-sized enterprises must be able to quickly identify and respond to customer needs; in order to do so, they need access to relevant market information. Technology also plays a key role in agility; in order to be agile, organizations must be able to rapidly adopt new technologies. And finally, business model innovation requires firms to experiment with new ways of doing business in order to find the most effective model for their particular context. Liu and Yang (2020) conclude that, "network resource can create an idiosyncratic competitive advantage for Agility-seeking small and medium-sized enterprises". In other words, by leveraging the power of networks, small and medium-sized enterprises can overcome the disadvantage of their size and lack of resources and become truly agile organizations. Thus, business agility is a critical competency for small businesses looking to create resilience in the face of uncertainty. Business agility is not only about being able to quickly change direction. It is also about being able to anticipate change and be proactive in crisis response. Business agility enables small businesses to not only survive, but also thrive in times of change. By being able to quickly adapt to market shifts and customer needs, small businesses can stay ahead of the competition and position themselves for long-term success.

3.4 Government Support

Government support can play a vital role in helping small businesses to create resilience. By providing financial assistance and other forms of support, government agencies can help small businesses to weather the storm during tough economic times. The global pandemic has had a devastating effect on businesses around the world. In response, many governments have put in place measures to support small businesses so they can continue operating and recover from the impact of COVID-19. For example, in the United States, the government has provided financial assistance through programs such as the Paycheck Protection Program and Economic Injury Disaster Loans. The Small Business Administration has also implemented a few changes to make it easier for small businesses to access credit and capital. In Canada, the government has provided the interest-free loans through the Canada Emergency Business Account, in order to help small businesses. The government has also deferred tax payments and provided rent relief for commercial tenants. In the United Kingdom, the government has created a number of initiatives to support small businesses, including the Coronavirus Business Interruption Loan Scheme and the Self-Employed Income Support Scheme. The government has also deferred VAT and income tax payments, and provided grants to help with business costs. These are just some of the many examples of how governments are supporting small businesses during this difficult time.

Financial support is particularly important, as it can help businesses to invest in new technologies and processes that can improve their sustainability. For example, Salem et al. (2021) discuss how the Egyptian government's support of businesses during the COVID-19 pandemic has helped to mitigating the negative impact on hotel employees. The authors explain that the government's decision to provide financial support to businesses has helped to keep many hotels afloat, which in turn has helped to protect jobs and incomes. In addition, the government has also provided training and support to hotel employees, helping them to adapt to new safety protocols and procedures. While these policies can certainly provide a much-needed lifeline for businesses, they also come with some risks (Kozeniauskas et al., 2020). For example, there is the danger that businesses will become reliant on government support, hampering their ability to compete in the long-term. There is also the risk that poorly designed policies will simply serve to delay the inevitable and end up prolonging the crisis. Further it should be noted that not all businesses will be able to take advantage of such support; in particular, those that are already facing financial difficulties are likely to struggle even more (Pu et al., 2021).

3.5 Entrepreneurial Well-being

In recent years, there has been a growing body of research on the relationship between well-being and entrepreneurship. This work has shown that entrepreneurs often have high levels of well-being, resilient personality traits, and a strong ability to bounce back from setbacks (Stephan et al., 2022). Entrepreneurial well-being is defined as "the experience of satisfaction, positive affect, infrequent negative affect, and psychological functioning in relation to developing, starting, growing, and running an entrepreneurial venture"(Wiklund et al., 2019, p. 579). Small business owners who experienced more mental health problems are less likely to reinvest in their businesses or to expand their businesses after the crisis (De Mel et al., 2008). This highlights the importance of mental health in business resilience after a major catastrophe. Positive affect has been found to be associated with increased psychological resilience (Xing & Sun, 2013). Individuals who experience frequent positive affective states are not only more successful, but also better able to deal with various challenges. This is because they actively build resources that help them cope with adversity. Positive affect therefore plays an important role in promoting psychological resilience. The study of people who witnessed the September 11th 2001 terrorist attacks demonstrates that those able to generate positive affect after crisis are more likely bounce back from it (Fredrickson et al., 2003).

Drawing from the neural mechanisms of resilience concept (Waugh et al., 2008), the amygdala is the part of our brain that responds most strongly to emotionally charged stimuli (e.g., a dangerous situation). The insula will stimulate in anticipation; it is always on alert for anything potentially threatening or anxiety-inducing (e.g., something dangerous about to happen). The orbitofrontal cortex becomes active when we expect a threat and deactivates if that same threat never actually materializes or subsides. This means individuals who have high levels positive affect are likely to find supportive meanings for adverse situations, while those on the other end must learn coping skills and develop stronger psychological resilience if they want better results when things get tough (Nath & Pradhan, 2012).

Evidently, there is a significant relationship between positive mental health and resilience (Srivastava, 2011). She defines positive mental health as a state of well-being in which an individual can realize his or her own abilities, cope with the normal stresses life throws at him/her and work productively. Resilience, on the other hand, is the ability to bounce back after adversity. This includes trauma, tragedy. and even significant sources of stress which would cause most people's lives to be dramatically altered for worse or better depending on their situation. Srivastava argues that positive mental health is essential for resilience, as it helps individuals to better cope with challenges and setbacks. Furthermore, she notes that resilient individuals are often able to draw on their positive mental health to bounce back from difficult experiences.

In conclusion, the importance of entrepreneurial well-being cannot be overstated. Entrepreneurs face a unique set of challenges that can take a toll on their mental health and well-being. However, by prioritizing their own well-being, entrepreneurs can build resilience and better cope with the ups and downs of entrepreneurship.Entrepreneurial well-being is not only important for individual entrepreneurs but also for the success of their ventures. Research has shown that entrepreneurs who prioritize their mental health are more likely to reinvest in their businesses and expand them after a crisis (De Mel et al., 2008). This means that investing in one's own well-being can also have positive effects on the success and growth potential of an entrepreneurial venture. Moreover, by promoting positive affect and psychological resilience, entrepreneurial well-being can help entrepreneurs navigate crises with greater ease. This translates into better decision-making during difficult times, which ultimately leads to stronger outcomes for both the entrepreneur and their business. In summary, while entrepreneurship is inherently challenging, it is possible to thrive as an entrepreneur while maintaining good mental health. By prioritizing self-care practices such as exercise routines or mindfulness practices, entrepreneurs can build resilience and develop the skills needed to overcome obstacles with confidence. Ultimately this will lead to greater success in both personal life as well as professional life.

4 Conclusion

COVID-19 has been a devastating blow to small businesses across the globe. While many factors have contributed to this staggering number, the most significant has been the shutdown of brick-and-mortar operations. For many small businesses, this has meant a complete loss of revenue. The concept of business resilience can help small businesses to cope with the impact of COVID-19 and other crisis situations. Business resilience is the ability of an organization to withstand and recover from disruptive events. It is about having the right policies and processes in place so that the businesses can quickly adapt to changing conditions and continue to operate effectively. This chapter discusses five core factors influence small business resilience during COVID-19 crisis. Diversification, financial resources, business agility competency, government support, and entrepreneurial well-being are all important factors that can help small businesses to cope with COVID crisis. Diversification helps businesses to have multiple revenue streams and not be reliant on one income source. This is especially important during a crisis like COVID where businesses may lose income from one source but still have other sources of revenue to fall back on. Financial resources give businesses the ability to weather a crisis like COVID without going under. Having access to financial resources can help businesses to pay their employees, keep their doors open, and continue operating during tough times.

Business agility competency helps businesses to be able to adapt quickly to change. In the case of COVID, businesses had to pivot quickly to online operations to survive. Those that were able to do so successfully were the ones that coped the best with the crisis. Government support is also crucial for small businesses during a time like this. The government has provided financial assistance and other forms of support to help businesses keep their doors open and employees paid. Lastly, entrepreneurial well-being is important because it helps business owners to stay positive and motivated during tough times. If business owners are feeling stressed, burnt out, or defeated, this will impact negatively on their business. However, if they are able to maintain their well-being, they will be in a better position to weather the storm and come out on the other side stronger than ever before.

References

Adekola, J., & Clelland, D. (2020). Two sides of the same coin: Business resilience and community resilience. *Journal of Contingencies and Crisis Management, 28*(1), 50–60.

Amann, B., & Jaussaud, J. (2012). Family and non-family business resilience in an economic downturn. *Asia Pacific Business Review, 18*(2), 203–223. https://doi.org/10.1080/13602381.2010.537057

Arbussa, A., Bikfalvi, A., & Marquès, P. (2017). Strategic agility-driven business model renewal: The case of an SME. *Management Decision, 55*(2), 271–293.

Bartik, A. W., Bertrand, M., Cullen, Z., Glaeser, E. L., Luca, M., & Stanton, C. (2020). The impact of COVID-19 on small business outcomes and expectations. *Proceedings of the National Academy of Sciences, 117*(30), 17656–17666. https://doi.org/10.1073/pnas.2006991117

Beech, N., Devins, D., Gold, J., & Beech, S. (2019). In the family way: An exploration of family business resilience. *International Journal of Organizational Analysis, 28*(1), 160–182.

Belitski, M., Guenther, C., Kritikos, A. S., & Thurik, R. (2022). Economic effects of the COVID-19 pandemic on entrepreneurship and small businesses. *Small Business Economics, 58*(2), 593–609.

Buffington, C., Dennis, C., Dinlersoz, E., Foster, L., & Klimek, S. (2020). *Measuring the effect of COVID-19 on U.S. small businesses: The small business pulse survey.* (Working Papers 20-16). Center for Economic Studies, U.S. Census Bureau.

Carlson, J. L., Haffenden, R. A., Bassett, G. W., Buehring, W. A., Collins III, M. J., Folga, S. M., et al. (2012). *Resilience: theory and application.* (No. ANL/DIS-12-1). Argonne National Lab. (ANL), Argonne, IL.

Chadwick, I. C., & Raver, J. L. (2020). Psychological resilience and its downstream effects for business survival in nascent entrepreneurship. *Entrepreneurship Theory and Practice, 44*(2), 233–255.

Chan, C. M. L., Teoh, S. Y., Yeow, A., & Pan, G. (2019). Agility in responding to disruptive digital innovation: Case study of an SME. *Information Systems Journal, 29*(2), 436–455.

De Mel, S., McKenzie, D., & Woodruff, C. (2008). Mental health recovery and economic recovery after the tsunami: High-frequency longitudinal evidence from Sri Lankan small business owners. *Social Science & Medicine, 66*(3), 582–595.

Eggers, F. (2020). Masters of disasters? Challenges and opportunities for SMEs in times of crisis. *Journal of Business Research, 116*, 199–208.

Fairlie, R., & Fossen, F. M. (2022). The early impacts of the COVID-19 pandemic on business sales. *Small Business Economics, 58*(4), 1853–1864.

Fletcher, D., & Sarkar, M. (2013). Psychological resilience: A review and critique of definitions, concepts, and theory. *European Psychologist, 18*(1), 12–23.

Fredrickson, B. L., Tugade, M. M., Waugh, C. E., & Larkin, G. R. (2003). What good are positive emotions in crisis? A prospective study of resilience and emotions following the terrorist attacks on the United States on September 11th, 2001. *Journal of Personality and Social Psychology, 84*(2), 365–376.

Ke, J.-y. F., Otto, J., & Han, C. (2022). Customer-country diversification and inventory efficiency: Comparative evidence from the manufacturing sector during the pre-pandemic and the COVID-19 pandemic periods. *Journal of Business Research, 148*(September), 292–303.

Kim, O., Parker, J. A., & Schoar, A. (2020). *Revenue collapses and the consumption of small business owners in the early stages of the COVID-19 pandemic.* (Working Paper No. 28151). National Bureau of Economic Research.

Korber, S., & McNaughton, R. B. (2017). Resilience and entrepreneurship: A systematic literature review. *International Journal of Entrepreneurial Behavior & Research, 24*(7), 1129–1154.

Kozeniauskas, N., Moreira, P., & Santos, C. (2020). *Covid-19 and firms: Productivity and government policies.* (Discussion Paper DP15156). Centre for Economic Policy Research.

Lee, J. E., Sudom, K. A., & Zamorski, M. A. (2013). Longitudinal analysis of psychological resilience and mental health in Canadian military personnel returning from overseas deployment. *Journal of Occupational Health Psychology, 18*(3), 327–337.

Liu, H.-M., & Yang, H.-F. (2020). Network resource meets organizational agility. *Management Decision, 58*(1), 58–75. https://doi.org/10.1108/MD-10-2017-1061

Nath, P., & Pradhan, R. K. (2012). Influence of positive affect on physical health and psychological well-being: Examining the mediating role of psychological resilience. *Journal of Health Management, 14*(2), 161–174.

Nyamrunda, F. C., & Freeman, S. (2021). Strategic agility, dynamic relational capability and trust among SMEs in transitional economies. *Journal of World Business, 56*(3), 101175.

Pu, G., Qamruzzaman, M., Mehta, A. M., Naqvi, F. N., & Karim, S. (2021). Innovative finance, technological adaptation and SMEs sustainability: The mediating role of government support during COVID-19 pandemic. *Sustainability, 13*(16), 9218.

Salem, I. E., Elbaz, A. M., Elkhwesky, Z., & Ghazi, K. M. (2021). The COVID-19 pandemic: The mitigating role of government and hotel support of hotel employees in Egypt. *Tourism Management, 85*(August), 104305.

Srivastava, K. (2011). Positive mental health and its relationship with resilience. *Industrial Psychiatry Journal, 20*(2), 75–76.

Stephan, U., Zbierowski, P., Pérez-Luño, A., Wach, D., Wiklund, J., Alba Cabañas, M., Barki, E., Benzari, A., Bernhard-Oettel, C., Boekhorst, J. A., Dash, A., Efendic, A., Eib, C., Hanard, P.-J., Iakovleva, T., Kawakatsu, S., Khalid, S., Leatherbee, M., Li, J., et al. (2022). Act or wait-and-see? Adversity, agility, and entrepreneur wellbeing across countries during the COVID-19 Pandemic. *Entrepreneurship Theory and Practice*. https://doi.org/10.1177/0391560321993587.

Troise, C., Corvello, V., Ghobadian, A., & O'Regan, N. (2022). How can SMEs successfully navigate VUCA environment: The role of agility in the digital transformation era. *Technological Forecasting and Social Change, 174*, 121227.

Waugh, C. E., Fredrickson, B. L., & Taylor, S. F. (2008). Adapting to life's slings and arrows: Individual differences in resilience when recovering from an anticipated threat. *Journal of Research in Personality, 42*(4), 1031–1046.

Wiklund, J., Nikolaev, B., Shir, N., Foo, M.-D., & Bradley, S. (2019). Entrepreneurship and well-being: Past, present, and future. *Journal of Business Venturing, 34*(4), 579–588.

Xing, C., & Sun, J.-m. (2013). The role of psychological resilience and positive affect in risky decision-making. *International Journal of Psychology, 48*(5), 935–943.

4

Forward Looking

Abstract Crisis management is a critical part of any business. How well a company responds to and manages a crisis can mean the difference between business survival and going under. Small businesses find themselves at a disadvantage when it comes to crisis management. They lack the resources of larger businesses and often do not have the same level of experience in dealing with crisis situations. Small businesses are also typically heavily reliant on continuous customer spending and cash flows. A sudden drop in consumer confidence can have a devastating effect on sales and revenue. Finally, small businesses often lack the formal structure and processes of larger organizations, making them more difficult to manage during a crisis. These characteristics can make it difficult for small businesses to respond effectively to a crisis, leading to potential financial losses and damage to their reputation. The best way to be prepared for a crisis is by understanding the importance of managing them properly. Small businesses will have higher chances at survival during tough times when they can leverage their knowledge and expertise in this field, which could help turn even an arduous situation into one that is manageable with some planning ahead. There are many factors to consider when it comes to crisis management, from having a plan in place to knowing how to communicate with stakeholders. In this chapter, some of the key elements of effective crisis management will be illustrated, and some tips on how small businesses can improve their approach will be offered.

Keywords Managing crisis • Crisis-preparedness • Stakeholder communication

1   Responding Now and Preparing for the Future

Crisis response strategies are important for small businesses because they can help a business recover from an unexpected event. A well-thought-out crisis response plan can help a business owner identify potential risks, plan for how to respond to them, and keep the business running smoothly during and after a crisis. Attribution theory is often viewed as a theoretical framework to explain the relationship between strategic responses and the crisis situation. This psychological theory seeks to explain individuals' sensemaking of the world around them based on three dimensions of locus, stability, and controllability (Fiske & Taylor, 1991). Those with an internal locus of control believe they can influence events and outcomes, while those who think outside themselves are more likely inclined toward external circumstances being beyond anyone's understanding. Stability refers to the extent people believe that factors are consistent over time. Those who believe that factors are stable think that they will continue to be influential in the future, while those who believe that factors are unstable think that they may change at any time. Controllability refers to the extent to which people believe they can manage or control situations. Those who believe that they can control events are more likely to take actions to influence them, while those who believe that they cannot control events are more likely to feel hopeless and helpless.

According to the attribution theory by social psychologists Fritz Heider and Harold Kelley in the 1950s, people tend to explain events by either internal or external causes. Internal attributions relate an event to someone's personal qualities, whereas external attributions relate an event to outside forces beyond their control. Internal attributions can be more detrimental as they may lead to self-blame and reduced self-esteem, while external attributions can be more beneficial as they may provide a sense of empowerment and optimism. During a crisis, individuals often search for a scapegoat to blame. This is a coping mechanism that allows them to deal with the crisis by attributing responsibility to someone or something else. To minimize the negative effects of this behavior, it is possible to use a crisis response strategy that alters how people view the crisis based on three different dimensions.

When faced with a crisis, it is important to understand the attribution theory and how people tend to attribute blame either internally or externally. However, simply understanding this theory may not be enough to effectively manage a crisis. In fact, there are five different themes of crisis response strategies—non-existent, distance, ingratiation, mortification, and suffering—that can help individuals or businesses navigate a crisis in the most effective way possible (Coombs, 1995). These strategies can be used to alter how people view the crisis and minimize negative impacts such as self-blame and reduced self-esteem. First, *nonexistence* strategy involves denying that a problem exists. For example, Johnson & Johnson denied that their talc power contained asbestos, despite a small trace of chrysotile asbestos contamination in a single bottle purchased from online retailer, and thousands of lawsuits alleging the talc power containing asbestos (Glenza, 2022). Nonexistence strategy can be effective in some cases, but it is often seen as disingenuous and can further damage the reputation of an organization. Second, *distance* strategy involves distancing oneself from the problem. It can help to reduce liability and protect the reputation of an organization. However, it can also be seen as cold and uncaring. *Ingratiation* strategy involves trying to make amends with those affected by the problem. It can be an effective way to repair relationships and rebuild trust. For example, a company might offer discounts or free products to customers who have been affected by a recall. This strategy can be helpful in rebuilding trust and goodwill, but it should be used carefully. Overuse of this strategy can backfire and make the company appear insincere or manipulative. *Mortification* strategy involves accepting responsibility for the problem and apologizing. It is often seen as the most honest and sincere way to respond to a crisis. For example, if a company's website crashes on the day of a big sale, the company might issue a public apology along with an explanation of what went wrong and what the company is doing to fix it. This can help calm angry customers and restore their trust in its brand. *Suffering* strategy involves accepting the negative consequences of the problem. It can be an effective way to show remorse and rebuild trust. For example, if a company has caused environmental damage, the company may accept responsibility and clean up the mess. This shows that the company is willing to take responsibility for its actions and is taking steps to fix the problem. However, this strategy can also be seen as weakness.

There is no one-size-fits-all answer to the question of how best to respond to a crisis. A recent work conducted among small businesses in Italy found that the most successful responses were tailored to the specific needs of the business and the type of crisis being faced (Campagnolo et al., 2022). This highlights the importance of flexible and adaptable responses in times of crisis. The authors believe that this type of research can help guide small businesses in developing their own customized responses to future crises. Crisis response is a process that businesses use to assess and respond to a crisis quickly and effectively. The goal of crisis response is to minimize the damage caused by the crisis and to ensure that the business can quickly resume operations. Crisis response plans should be designed before a crisis occurs so that everyone knows what their roles and responsibilities are.

There are common steps in the crisis response that have been shown in the prior chapters. The first step is assessment. This involves taking stock of the situation and determining the extent of the damage. For example, after a hurricane, a business owner would need to assess the damage to their property and inventory. The second step is response. This is where the business owner takes action to address the crisis. For example, they may contact their insurance company or begin making repairs. The third step is recovery. This is the process of returning to normal operations. For example, a business may reopen its doors or start offering services again. The fourth and final step is lessons learned. This is where the business owner reflects on the experience and identifies ways to prevent or mitigate future crises. By taking these four steps, small businesses can increase their chances of surviving a crisis.

Active responses are those that seek to directly address the crisis, while *passive* responses seek to avoid or downplay the crisis. *Proactive* responses, meanwhile, seek to prevent future crises from occurring. Claeys and Coombs (2019) argue that organizations often choose suboptimal responses to crises because they fail to take into account the different costs and benefits of each option. For example, an organization might choose a passive response because it is less expensive than an active response, but this could backfire if the crisis worsens, and the passive response is seen as ineffective. Similarly, an organization might choose a proactive response to prevent future crises, but this could also be costly and may not actually prevent any future crises from occurring. Therefore, to improve decision-making in crises, organizations should consider the costs and benefits of each option before deciding that they should consult with experts when they make decisions about crisis response options, and that they should review their decisions after a crisis has occurred in order to learn from their mistakes.

Regardless of their size, businesses must prioritize crisis-preparedness as crucial reading material. This is especially true for small businesses, who can learn from past failures to better equip themselves for worst-case scenarios. While having established procedures in place for managing crises is important, it is equally important for organizations to continuously learn and improve upon these procedures (Carmeli & Schaubroeck, 2008). This is a crucial point: no matter how well prepared an organization is, there will always be room for improvement. The best way to learn and improve is to constantly review past failures and try to learn from them. There are a few steps that small businesses can take to develop a crisis plan. First, they should identify the risks that could affect their business. This could include anything from natural disasters to economic downturns. Once the risks have been identified, the next step is to develop strategies to mitigate those risks. This could involve things like diversifying your customer base or having emergency funding in place. Once the plans are in place, it is important to regularly review and update them. This will ensure that they are still relevant and effective in the event of a crisis.

2 Communicating with Relevant Stakeholders

When it comes to communicating during a crisis, speed is of the essence. It is important to get the message out quickly and accurately, using multiple channels if necessary. Social media can be a valuable tool for getting information out quickly. The rise of social media has allowed organizations to reach a wider audience with their messages during a crisis (Cheng, 2018). Additionally, social media provides a more immediate way of communication than traditional forms such as television or radio. This is because social media platforms allow organizations to send out updates and information as soon as it becomes available, without waiting for a scheduled news bulletin. In addition, social media allows organizations to directly engage with their audiences, which can help to build trust and credibility. For example, during the 2017 hurricanes that hit the US, the American Red Cross used social media to provide real-time updates on the situation and to answer questions from the public.

Crisis communication should not just be about disseminating information. It should also aim to reassure employees, customers, and other stakeholders that the company is doing everything it can to resolve the situation. An effective crisis communication strategy will take all of these factors into account and provide a roadmap for how to deal with a crisis effectively. There is the interplay between information form and source of crisis communication (Liu et al., 2011). Using content analysis to examine how 1280 Chinese Internet users responded to two types of crisis communication messages (i.e., apology and denial) from two sources (i.e., organization and government), the results indicated that when the message was an apology, it was more effective coming from the organization than the government. However, when the message was a denial, it was more effective coming from the government than the organization. These findings suggest that the source of the message is an important factor to consider when developing a crisis communication strategy.

Crisis communication is essential in relation to the public perception of COVID-19 risk. A recent study shows that the way information is presented can have a significant impact on how people perceive risks

(Malecki et al., 2021). For example, if information about the COVID-19 is presented in a positive light, people are more likely to see the risk as manageable and take precautions. However, if information is presented in a negative light, people are more likely to see the risk as unmanageable and take no precautions. This suggests that it is important for those in charge of communicating information about the COVID-19 to be careful about how they present risks. It is also important to ensure that accurate and up-to-date information is being communicated. Inaccurate or outdated information can cause people to underestimate the risk and make them less likely to take precautions. When developing a crisis communication plan, small businesses owners may consider context, audience, and message (Mansor & KaderAli, 2017). The context refers to the specific situation in which the crisis occurs. The audience includes all of the stakeholders who will be affected by the crisis. The message is the information that companies want to communicate to the audience. Taking these three factors into account can help small business owners develop an effective crisis communication strategy. When companies adopt a pro-social stance, consumers are more likely to remain loyal and continue doing business with them. Additionally, companies that provide clear and concise information about the crisis are more likely to regain trust and confidence (Ranković et al., 2011).

Effectively communicating during a crisis can be difficult, but it is essential in order to minimize the damage caused by the event. For example, in the summer of 2016, three different crises—the shooting at the Pulse nightclub, the alligator attack at a local resort, and the outbreak of Zika virus—struck the Orlando area within a span of six weeks. This presented a unique challenge for local hotels, who had to communicate with guests and potential guests during a time of crisis. The hotels generally followed the stages of crisis communication prescribed by Situational Crisis Communication Theory (SCCT). SCCT was first proposed by W. Timothy Coombs in 1999, in response to what he saw as a need for a more contextualized approach to crisis communication. Prior to SCCT, most crisis communication models had focused on the organization's message and how best to get that message across. Coombs argued that this was too narrow a focus; instead, he proposed that an effective crisis communication strategy must take into account the specific situation in which the organization finds itself. SCCT has three main components: pre-crisis, crisis, and post-crisis. In the pre-crisis stage, the hotels in Orlando used Twitter to provide information about hurricane preparedness; in the crisis stage, they provided updates on damage and closures; in the post-crisis stage, they posted reopening dates and special offers. The hotels used a mix of preventive, defensive, and accommodative strategies, which helped to minimize the negative impact of these crises on the city's tourism industry (Barbe & Pennington-Gray, 2018).

3 Maintaining Sanity

Small business owners are among the most vulnerable groups during the COVID-19 pandemic (Beland et al., 2020; Yue & Cowling, 2021). When the pandemic hit in 2020, many small business owners found themselves under immense pressure. Not only were they facing the challenges of running a business during a global crisis, but they also had to contend with the personal impact of the virus. In a recent study, Torrès et al. (2021) explored the health perception of small business owners during the COVID outbreak. Small business owners reported negative impacts on their physical and mental health, with many citing higher level of psychological distress. The pandemic has also taken a toll on business owners' finances, with many reporting reduced incomes and increased costs. This has had a knock-on effect on their ability to maintain a healthy lifestyle, with many respondents reporting that they have been unable to exercise or eat as healthily as they would like. Small business owners are also at an increased risk of burnout during the COVID-19 crisis. The study surveyed 477 entrepreneurs and found that nearly 30% of respondents were at a high risk of burnout (Torrès et al., 2022). This is not surprising, as small business owners have been under immense pressure during the pandemic. They have had to contend with diminished demand, supply chain disruptions, and strict government restrictions. In addition, many have had to pivot their businesses in order to stay afloat. The constant stress and uncertainty has taken a toll on their mental and physical health.

As small business owners navigate the challenges of the COVID-19 pandemic, it is essential that they maintain a sense of self-efficacy to protect their mental health. This is because self-efficacy plays a mediating role in the relationship between beliefs about COVID and stress levels (Meyer et al., 2022). In other words, beliefs about the pandemic can impact how small business owners feel about their ability to cope with the stress of the situation. The study found that self-efficacy was highest among those who believed that the pandemic would have a negative impact on their business. This may be due to the fact that these individuals felt more capable of taking steps to protect their businesses from the effects of the pandemic. Alternatively, it could be that these individuals were simply more realistic about the situation and less likely to experience cognitive dissonance.

The COVID-19 pandemic has also exacerbated existing gender inequality in small business sector. The pandemic has had a disproportionately negative impact on female small business owners, as compared to men small business owners, especially in the hospitality and retail sectors. In addition, women are more likely to work from home, which has become increasingly difficult during the pandemic (Graeber et al., 2021). The crisis such as COVID-19 pandemic also impacted on the wellbeing of small business owners, leading to higher number of Hikikomori-like symptom, such as social withdrawal, fatigue, and sleep problems (Watabe et al., 2022). Hikikomori is a Japanese term used to describe people who withdraw from social life and isolate themselves at home.

Small businesses face numerous challenges, and unexpected crises can make things even more stressful. That's why it's crucial for business owners to maintain their sanity during these difficult times. By staying calm and focused, they can make clear-headed decisions that will benefit their business in the long run. Here are some reasons why maintaining sanity is essential for small businesses, especially during times of crisis:

1. Better decision-making: Stress and panic can impair rational decision-making abilities. By maintaining small business owners' sanity, they will be able to approach problems with a clear mind and make decisions based on logic and reason.

2. Improved communication: Effective communication with employees, customers, and other stakeholders is essential during a crisis. Being level-headed will help small business owners convey information clearly and calmly, which will inspire confidence in those around them.
3. Reduced risk of burnout: Running a small business is challenging work that can take a toll on mental health. However, by taking care of small business owners' mental well-being and maintaining their sanity, they will reduce the risk of burnout and be better equipped to handle any challenges that come their way.

Overall, maintaining sanity is vital for small businesses coping with crises. By staying calm and focused, business owners can make better decisions, communicate more effectively with others, and avoid burnout. Crises are an inevitable part of business. No matter how well small business owners plan or how strong their business is, there will always be times when small business owners face with a potentially damaging situation. While small businesses owners cannot always prevent a crisis from happening, they can take steps to minimize the impact it has on their business. By developing a crisis prevention and preparedness strategy, small business owners can ensure that their company is better equipped to handle whatever comes.

4 Conclusion

The world is still reeling from the effects of the COVID-19 pandemic. Businesses have been forced to shut down, and millions of people have lost their jobs. The economic and human toll of the pandemic has been immense. Now, as countries have reopened their economies, there is a pressing need to find a balance between health and economic factors. The process of reopening a small business after a prolonged shutdown is not a simple one, and it requires careful planning and execution (Pronk & Kassler, 2020). Small businesses have learned many valuable lessons from past crises, including how to respond to a crisis, prepare for the future, communicate effectively, and maintain their sanity during difficult times. It is the importance for small businesses to respond quickly and effectively to a crisis. Whether it is a natural disaster or an economic downturn, small businesses must be prepared to take action in order to minimize the impact on their operations. This includes having a solid plan in place for dealing with emergencies, as well as maintaining open lines of communication with employees, customers, and other stakeholders. Another key lesson that small businesses must prepare for the future. This means not only having contingency plans in place for potential crises but also investing in technologies and processes that can help them stay resilient in the face of adversity. Effective communication is also critical during a crisis. Small businesses must be transparent and honest with their stakeholders about what's happening and what steps they're taking to address the situation. Finally, maintaining sanity during a crisis is essential for both business owners and employees alike. It is important to prioritize self-care and mental health during difficult times. This may involve taking breaks when needed, seeking support from friends and family members, or even working with a therapist or counselor to manage stress levels.

References

Barbe, D., & Pennington-Gray, L. (2018). Using situational crisis communication theory to understand Orlando hotels' Twitter response to three crises in the summer of 2016. *Journal of Hospitality and Tourism Insights, 1*(3), 258–275.

Beland, L.-P., Fakorede, O., & Mikola, D. (2020). Short-term effect of COVID-19 on self-employed workers in Canada. *Canadian Public Policy, 46*(S1), S66–S81.

Campagnolo, D., Gianecchini, M., Gubitta, P., Leonelli, S., & Tognazzo, A. (2022). SMEs facing crisis: Ideal response or equifinal reactions? In *Business under crisis volume I* (pp. 63–84). Springer.

Carmeli, A., & Schaubroeck, J. (2008). Organizational crisis-preparedness: The importance of learning from failures. *Long Range Planning, 41*(2), 177–196.

Cheng, Y. (2018). How social media is changing crisis communication strategies: Evidence from the updated literature. *Journal of Contingencies and Crisis Management, 26*(1), 58–68.

Claeys, A.-S., & Coombs, W. T. (2019). Organizational crisis communication: Suboptimal crisis response selection decisions and behavioral economics. *Communication Theory, 30*(3), 290–309.

Coombs, W. T. (1995). Choosing the right words: The development of guidelines for the selection of the "appropriate" crisis-response strategies. *Management Communication Quarterly, 8*(4), 447–476.

Fiske, S. T., & Taylor, S. E. (1991). *Social cognition* (2nd ed.). McGraw-Hill.

Glenza, J. (Producer). (2022). Johnson & Johnson recalls baby powder after asbestos found. https://www.theguardian.com/business/2019/oct/18/johnson-johnson-baby-powder-recall-asbestos

Graeber, D., Kritikos, A. S., & Seebauer, J. (2021). COVID-19: A crisis of the female self-employed. *Journal of Population Economics, 34*(4), 1141–1187.

Heinze, I. (2022). Crisis management in SMEs from a leadership perspective. In S. Durst & T. Henschel (Eds.), *Crisis management for small and medium-sized enterprises (SMEs)* (pp. 143–164). Springer.

Liu, B. F., Austin, L., & Jin, Y. (2011). How publics respond to crisis communication strategies: The interplay of information form and source. *Public Relations Review, 37*(4), 345–353.

Malecki, K. M., Keating, J. A., & Safdar, N. (2021). Crisis communication and public perception of COVID-19 risk in the era of social media. *Clinical Infectious Diseases, 72*(4), 697–702.

Mansor, F., & KaderAli, N. N. (2017). Crisis management, crisis communication, and consumer purchase intention post-crisis. *Global Business & Management Research, 9*(4S), 60–79.

Meyer, N., Niemand, T., Davila, A., & Kraus, S. (2022). Correction: Biting the bullet: When self-efficacy mediates the stressful effects of COVID-19 beliefs. *PLOS ONE, 17*(3), e0265330.

Parnell, J. A. (2021). An ounce of prevention: What promotes crisis readiness and how does it drive firm performance? *American Business Review, 24*(1), 90–113.

Pronk, N. P., & Kassler, W. J. (2020). Balancing health and economic factors when reopening business in the age of COVID-19. *Journal of Occupational and Environmental Medicine, 62*(9), e540–e541.

Ranković, L., Stefanović, I., Prokić, S., & Janičić, R. (2011). Effects of crisis communication strategies on the behavior of consumers. *Industrija, 39*(4), 307–329.

Torrès, O., Benzari, A., Fisch, C., Mukerjee, J., Swalhi, A., & Thurik, R. (2022). Risk of burnout in French entrepreneurs during the COVID-19 crisis. *Small*

Business Economics, 58(2), 717–739. https://doi.org/10.1007/s11187-021-00516-2

Torrès, O., Fisch, C., Mukerjee, J., Lasch, F., & Thurik, R. (2021). Health perception of French SME owners during the 2020 COVID-19 pandemic. *International Review of Entrepreneurship, 19*(2), 151–168.

Watabe, M., Kubo, H., Horie, K., Katsuki, R., Yamakawa, I., Sakamoto, S., & Kato, T. A. (2022). Effects of COVID-19 on mental health in business: Increasing the hikikomori-like workers in Japan. In A. O. J. Kwok, M. Watabe, & S. G. M. Koh (Eds.), *COVID-19 and the evolving business environment in Asia: The hidden impact on the economy, business and society* (pp. 189–204). Springer Nature Singapore.

Yue, W., & Cowling, M. (2021). The Covid-19 lockdown in the United Kingdom and subjective well-being: Have the self-employed suffered more due to hours and income reductions? *International Small Business Journal, 39*(2), 93–108.

Index

A

Accessing social capital for small businesses, 31–33

C

Cognitive social capital, 30–31
Communicating with relevant stakeholders, 64–66
COVID-19 impact on small businesses, 42–43
Crisis level and organizational impacts, 5–7
Crisis sensemaking among small businesses, 19–23
Crisis stages
 individual perspective, 4
 organizational perspective, 5

D

Defining crisis, 2–4

F

Factors contribute to small business resilience, 47–55
 business agility competency, 50–51
 diversification, 48–49
 entrepreneurial well-being, 53–55
 financial resources, 49–50
 government support, 51–53

M

Maintaining sanity, 66–68
Multidisciplinary view on crisis, 7–9
 crisis from a psychological perspective, 7–9

Multidisciplinary view on crisis (*cont.*)
   crisis from a technological-structural perspective, 9
   organizational sensemaking of crisis, 10–12

P

Pitfalls in developing a business continuity planning strategy, 35–36

R

Responding now and preparing for the future, 60–63

The role of culture on sensemaking of crisis, 12–13

S

Small businesses are more vulnerable to crises, 18–19
Small businesses' business continuity management, 33–36
Small businesses resilience, 43–47
Small businesses respond on natural crisis, 23–27
Social capital as a resource for managing crisis, 27–33
Strategizing business continuity planning, 34–35

Printed by Printforce, United Kingdom